Delroy Hall

GW00646656

Foundations

───◆───

A Concise
History/Doctrine

Center for Biblical Leadership

White Wing Publishing House

Tennessee • Peru • Mexico • Guatemala
Philippines • Dominican Republic • India

ACD
1998

Foundations–A Concise History/Doctrine
Copyright ©1998
Published by White Wing Publishing House and Press
P. O. Box 3000
Cleveland, TN 37320-3000
(423) 559-5425 • 1-800-221-5027
All rights reserved
Cover Illustration: Perry Horner
First Published, 1998

ISBN 1-889-505-26-9

Preface

This foundations course of the Center for Biblical Leadership is presented with the hope that it will provide a basic knowledge of the principles to be embraced by those who are committed to Jesus Christ. We acknowledge freely His headship of the church He is building and we are dedicated to follow Him faithfully.

Being rather broad in scope there is not an attempt to deal with many of the specifics which subsequently it will be necessary to explore more fully. It will be revised and updated from time to time to assure current relevance to the needs of our people.

We sincerely appreciate all the research and work that has been done in the preparation of this foundations course. It is presented with the prayer that it will contribute to a more knowledgeable and a more competent leadership for God's people, as a foundational tool.

This course could be valuable locally for group or individual study. May God's grace add richness to what we are presenting here which will make our thrust into the harvest more effective.

BILLY D. MURRAY
General Overseer

Foreword

Students of history will know that the majority of historical writing is deliberately coldly factual and non-interpretative. It is also usual to find two histories from a Christian perspective; there is what we call "The History of Christianity" which seeks to show how the new life, the life divine is preserved by the government of our Lord Jesus, who said, ". . . The words that I speak to you are spirit, and they are life." Then there is what we may call "The History of the Church," that is, of human institutions, forms, doctrines, and actions.

In this concise history of the Church of God of Prophecy, the writer, Wade H. Phillips has taken a different approach to the one normally taken by the detached secular historian. In this modern age, it has become almost an axiom of the historian that he must treat his subject "scientifically," and above all impersonally, concealing to the last degree his own personal convictions. He should write as if possessed of neither conscience (except for the establishment of cold historical truth) nor faith. As a strict academic exercise this method may possess merits, but is unlikely to provide the reader with much that is called interest.

From a period that produced many colorful but devout men of God, the reader will have their interest peaked by this Concise History of the Church of God of Prophecy. It is my belief the writer's years of research and collection of historical documents has been used effectively to create a panoramic view of the main events and personalities that will sure to appeal to the sympathy of the inquiring mind. The result is a short but important analysis distinguished by the potency of its vivid portraiture and detailed narration of some of the more critically defining moments in the church's history. What we have is an insight into the convictions, the passions, the interest that drove men on, and a noble attempt to understand the tide of human life in which the events took place. In all of this, the reader will get the impression that the writer is not simply dissecting the dry bones of men of bygone years, but that he is stirred by the events on which he has chosen to write.

Inevitably in a work of this nature, there will be issues raised that will cause some to question the accuracy and veracity of the source information. In an effort to show that what has been said is more than idle speculation, or rhetorical amplification, the writer has gone to great lengths to show source credibility through extensive and comprehensive endnotes. It is the evidence provided by these notes— some 370 references—together with a detailed bibliography that should enable the student to study the spiritual landscape of the time. Students who so desire could use these sources to effect a minute study of certain events in order to better understand the driving force which impelled the individual men, thus in specific instances, acquire a more sympathetic appreciation and reproduction of their largely forgotten past.

This is not a study of the missiological endeavors of the church, but rather an analysis of the main events and leadership developments that has unquestionably shaped and defined what the church has become today. There is no intent to imply that the history of missionary achievements has been an insignificant factor in the church's development. From the international composition of the church presently, one can clearly see the dramatic impact of the church's commitment to missions. Some attempt has been made to show how the work of the church spread around the world. However, a document of this nature could hardly be called concise if we were to include the details of each of these developments. Since the historical development of the church in every country is special, it is hoped that this particular course would lay the foundation for national or regional treatise of the subject matter.

Oswill E. Williams, Director
Leadership Development and Discipleship Ministries

Introduction

The Church of God of Prophecy traces its founding back to the New Testament when Jesus " . . . calleth unto him whom he would . . . and he ordained twelve, that they should be with him, and that he might send them forth to preach" (Mark 3:13,14). These Twelve formed the nucleus of the church that Christ taught and commissioned to publish His gospel. On the Day of Pentecost the church (already set in order) was empowered by the Spirit to fulfill the commission given by its risen Lord. Thereafter, the apostles laid more fully the foundation of the church, and defined its doctrine, government, and institutions. As such, the church is distinguished from the eternal and heavenly kingdom of God. The latter is God's direct rule in men's hearts, whereas the church is His instrumental rule—that is to say, God ruling through Spirit-filled men.[1] The Kingdom is therefore morally perfect, the church imperfect.[2] The church on earth is thus understood to be the visible and corporate body of Christ, with a definite origin in history and a divinely appointed eschatology.[3] Its future as well as its past has been foreordained by God and is revealed through the prophets and apostles in the Scriptures. It is therefore the church of prophecy.

Prophetically, the church was predicted to apostatize (Isaiah 60:2; Zechariah 14:6-7; Jude 4; et al).[4] After Jesus' ascension the apostles warned of the church's fall and its consequences (Acts 20:29; 2 Thessalonians 2:1-4; 2 Peter 2-3; Jude 3-19; et al). Jesus Himself made a special appearance to warn of the church's impending apostasy (Revelation 1-3). Historically, after the passing of the apostles, the church's spiritual vitality and vision of God's eternal purpose gradually diminished. This fall climaxed with the "marriage" of church and state at the Council of Nicea in A.D. 325.[5] Following the Council of Nicea the apostate church plunged deeper and deeper into error and spiritual darkness. This period was described by Isaiah: "For behold darkness shall cover the earth, and gross darkness the people" (Isaiah 60:2). Nevertheless, the church was prophesied to be restored to its prestine power and glory. Again, Isaiah prophesied, "Arise, shine, for thy light is come and the glory of the Lord is risen upon thee" (60:1).[6] This restoration was in order for the church to fulfill its eternal purpose (Ephesians 3:9-11; Revelation 19:7). The church's restoration—in gospel purity and Pentecostal power—was described by the prophets as the "latter rain" (Joel 2:23; Zechariah 10:1) and "evening light" (Zechariah 14:7); and it was envisioned in "glory" and "brightness" (Isaiah 60:1-3).

The modern history of the church is rooted in the religious movements that swept Europe and England in the sixteenth and seventeenth centuries. It is more particularly a legacy of what some historians have called the "radical reformation." Groups such as Anabaptists, Mennonites, Baptists, and Quakers contended that the primary reformers—Luther, Calvin, and Zwingli—had fallen short of a complete restoration of God's church. These radical reformers, therefore, sought to fully restore the church upon deep spiritual experiences, personal piety, strict moral discipline, and a separation of church and state.[7]

When groups of radical reformers immigrated to America in the seventeenth and eighteenth centuries, their ideas found fertile soil and flourished in the colonies. Personal piety and congregational discipline were to them the hallmarks of the true church, in contrast to state-supported churches with rigid ecclesiastical hierarchies that enforced human traditions over the Word of God. Great revivals, some marked by Pentecostal manifestations, occurred among the radical reform groups, especially the Baptists and the followers of George Whitefield and John Wesley. Following in this tradition, the forefathers of the Church of God of Prophecy viewed their work as both a continuation and restoration of the apostolic church.[8]

Contents

Introduction

Concise History of the Church of God of Prophecy

Learning Goals and Objectives:

After reading the lesson material, and carefully completing the questions in a studious manner, the individual will have acquired sufficient knowledge, and should be able to demonstrate an understanding of the Church of God of Prophecy by:

- explaining the biblical origins of the church, its empowerment on the Day of Pentecost, and its foreordained role in history.

- describing the significance of R. G. Spurling, W. F. Bryant, A. J. Tomlinson, the Christian Union, and the Holiness Church at Camp Creek to the formation of the Church of God of Prophecy.

- discussing the importance of the church's latter-day Pentecostal identity.

- describing the development of church government as this was realized through the General Assembly, the office of General Overseer, and the appointment of state overseers.

- summarizing the early missionary endeavors, and the subsequent spread of the church into more than 90 countries of the world.

- identifying the factors, central issues and the individuals that played a major role in the 1922-23 disruption.

- explaining the continuation of the church after 1923 as this unfolded in the development of Fields of the Wood, the church flag, Bible Training Camp, and the death of A. J. Tomlinson.

- identifying the main features, struggles and victories under the leadership of M. A. Tomlinson.

- discussing the crises and causation factors for the changes and the refocusing of the church's essential mission, in relation to the leadership actions and vision articulated by Billy D. Murray, after his selection as General Overseer.

Time Line	Beginnings and Early Developments
1884	Richard G. Spurling reacted against creedalism
1886	Christian Union formed
1889	Barney Creek congregation ceased to function
1891	Elder Spurling died
1896	Revival in Monroe County
1902	Holiness Church at Camp Creek born
1903	A. J. Tomlinson joined the church
1904	Tomlinson moved to Cleveland, TN
1906	First General Assembly in the home of J. C. Murphy
1908	G. B. Cashwell preached Pentecostal message at the General Assembly
1909	Tomlinson selected to serve as General Moderator of General Assembly
1913	State Overseer appointments made by General Overseer
1914	Tomlinson appointed as General Overseer for life
1916	Resolution to create a twelve-man council of elders

Beginnings and Early Developments

Unit One

Christian Union

Beginning in 1884, Richard G. Spurling, a former licentiate in the Baptist church, and his father, Richard Spurling (1810-1891),[9] an ordained Baptist minister, reacted against the prevailing creedalism among the Baptists of their day.[10] The "Landmark Movement" led by J. R. Graves had permeated the Southern Baptist denomination with an exclusivistic view of "true" Baptist churches, claiming to be able to trace their roots through an unbroken chain of succession to John the Baptist.[11] Richard G. Spurling, having been born and reared in the Landmark tradition, began about 1884 to question the doctrine of a historical line succession by which the true church could be identified. But he particularly loathed the bigotry and rigid creedalism that characterized Landmark exclusivism.[12] After two years of travailing prayer and intense studies in the Bible and church history, Spurling developed a restorationist view of church history. He believed that such biblical motifs as the "latter rain" and "evening light" justified his interpretation.[13] Accordingly, the New Testament church had apostatized with the "marriage" of church and state at the Council of Nicea in A.D. 325.[14] This "unholy alliance" marked the beginning of a long period of spiritual and ecclesiastical darkness. The apostasy deepened in the ensuing centuries within the Roman Catholic system, particularly with the rise of the papacy.[15] Moreover, though the efforts of the Protestant reformers were noble in attempting to correct the antichrist practices of the papal system, Spurling maintained that they had failed to restore the New Testament church and, in fact, perpetuated many of Rome's errors in the state churches that followed them.[16]

Consequently, on August 19, 1886, after a challenging message by Richard G. Spurling, his wife and aging father with six others came forward and covenanted together to effect what they believed to be a true restoration of the apostolic church.[17] They called it "Christian Union" and constituted it upon principles remarkably comparable to sixteenth-century Anabaptists. The group agreed to free themselves "from all (man) made creeds and traditions . . . to take the New Testament, or law of Christ, as their only rule of faith and practice, [and to give] each other equal rights and privileges to read and interpret [the Scriptures for themselves as their consciences may dictate]."[18] Further, they agreed to "sit together as the church of God to transact business . . . "[19] These actions were inspired by the vision and conviction of Richard G. Spurling, with the support of his aging father, whose status as an ordained Baptist minister was believed to have legitimatized their independent action.[20] Richard G. Spurling was then appointed as the pastor of "the infant church of God," and two weeks later his father ordained him with the consent of the congregation.[21] However, while still offering moral support for his son's ministry and vision, the elder Spurling made peace with and returned to his Baptist church at Holly Springs shortly after the formation of Christian Union,[22] leaving his son alone to carry on the work of restoration and the ecumenical vision for Christian Union. A widower since 1878, the elder Spurling married again in 1887 and died in 1891.[23]

Richard G. Spurling (1857-1935)[24] succeeded in establishing at least two more Christian Union congregations in Monroe County, Tennessee, after the mother congregation at Barney Creek ceased to function in 1889.[25] Later he organized at least one congregation in Polk County near the Cherokee County line on the Hiwassee River.[26] Spurling's doctrine of the independence of each person to decide for himself the interpretation of Scripture, and the corresponding independence of each local congregation[27], coupled with his own lack of leadership ability, made it difficult, if not impossible, for him to fulfill the ideal for Christian Union. He struggled to maintain the congregation that he was pastoring on the Hiwassee River in Polk County, while the other congregations that he had organized in Monroe County went more or less their own way under the leadership of other men.[28] By 1902 Spurling's congregation in Polk County had dispersed, while the Monroe County congregations continued as struggling independent bodies.[29]

The Holiness Transformation

Beginning in 1895, portions of North and South Carolina, northern Georgia, and southeastern Tennessee became agitated by the radical wing of the Holiness movement. Benjamin Hardin Irwin had come south from the midwest and greatly affected the region with his "fire-baptized" holiness message.[30] The congregations that Spurling had organized were swept into the movement, thus moving them away from the general characteristics of Baptists to the tenets of radical holiness.[31] Spurling himself accepted holiness, but endeavored to modify the fanaticism that tended to characterize Irwin's movement. Those who claimed "fire-baptisms" were often difficult to manage, and thus Spurling struggled more than ever to maintain order and discipline among his followers. In the Spring of 1896, in Cherokee County, North Carolina, about five miles from Spurling's congregation on the Hiwassee River in Polk County, and fifteen from the Christian Union congregations in Monroe County, an Irwin-influenced revival broke out.[32] The principal leaders of this revival were William ("Billy") Martin [1862-1943], a Methodist from Coker Creek, Joseph ("Joe") M. Tipton [1853-1923], Elias Milton McNabb [1860-1945], and William ("Billy") Hamby [1856-1908], all Baptists from Monroe County. These men had been acquainted or connected with Spurling and his work in Monroe County from the beginning.[33]

W. F. Bryant, Jr.(1863-1949), a Baptist deacon, was drawn into the Holiness movement during the revival in Cherokee County.[34] He was a member of the Liberty Baptist Church, the mother church of the Pleasant Hill congregation which had revoked Spurling's license and excluded him in 1884.[35] Eventually he became the leader of the group in the Camp Creek area.[36] Great persecution followed Bryant's group in the succeeding years. They were barred from using the Shearer Schoolhouse for services, and finally forced to hold services in private homes after violent ranters burned to the ground the log building they had erected for worship.[37] It was during the meetings in private homes between 1896-1901 that the Holy Spirit began to fall miraculously upon seekers hungry for a deeper experience in God. Manifestations of the Spirit resembling apostolic Christianity characterized their meetings, and apparently many of the recipients spoke in tongues.[38] These manifestations, however, were considered part and parcel to the experience of entire sanctification, which, since the time of John Fletcher, had been referred to as "the baptism of the Holy Ghost."[39] The Baptist churches in the area disfellowshipped all those "harboring the modern theory of sanctification," maintaining it to be "a dangerous heresy."[40] Persecution, violent at times, continued, with the opponents of holiness "wreaking havoc" on Bryant's loosely-formed band. Oppression from the outside, coupled with the lack of order and discipline on the inside, nearly devastated Bryant's group. By 1902 the little band had dwindled to only about 20 persons.[41]

Had it not been for the counsel and influence of Richard G. Spurling, Bryant and his company of believers might have vanished from history. After several unsuccessful attempts, Spurling finally persuaded Bryant on May 15, 1902 to organize in order for the work to survive. Consequently, the Holiness Church at Camp Creek was born with 16 charter members.[42] Spurling was selected by the congregation as pastor and Bryant was duly ordained as a deacon. In this manner, Spurling's vision for the restoration of God's church was perpetuated through Bryant and his struggling band; and, at that juncture, the church of God took upon it a holiness distinctive. Even so, the work continued to struggle. Spurling's view of the church remained influenced by certain Landmark concepts, namely, that local congregations were independent of each other, fellowshipping only on the basis of mutual love rather than a corporate government.[43] Any form of centralized authority or infringement upon individual congregations was vehemently resisted.[44] This view isolated the little holiness band within a dominion of Baptist churches; which, coupled with a lack of leadership, stunted the growth and development of the church. But this was all to be changed in the following year with the addition of a dynamic and cheerful new leader by the name of A. J. Tomlinson.

Tomlinson (1865-1943) had been reared, educated, and converted in the Quaker tradition. About 1892 he experienced the "double cure" of entire sanctification and began to cultivate holiness in his personal life.[45] But he remained restless and dissatisfied with his church affiliation.[46] In 1899 he came to the Appalachian Mountains as a missionary under the auspices of the American Bible and American Tract Societies.[47] He befriended Spurling, Bryant, and the Holiness Church at Camp Creek, and became impressed by Spurling's doctrine of the church.[48] On June 13, 1903, after a period of agonizing prayer and a personal revelation from God, Tomlinson united with the group.[49] Spurling administered to him the church's covenant and extended the "right hand of fellowship," which Tomlinson accepted with the understanding that "it is" the church of God of the Bible.[50] This event was held sacred by Tomlinson for the rest of his life. After years of religious wandering, he had finally found his niche in which to work for God.

Tomlinson's leadership potential was readily recognized by Spurling and the others, and he was immediately selected as pastor of the Camp Creek congregation.[51] The former Quaker was now driven by a sense of mission as never before. That year 14 members were added to the little flock, including M. S. Lemons.[52] In December 1904 Tomlinson moved to Cleveland and centered his activities there, traveling by rail and foot to evangelize and establish churches.[53]

The Pentecostal Transformation

A. J. Tomlinson, like many in the Camp Creek congregation, leaned toward Pentecostalism even before the turn of the twentieth century. Indeed, many of the church's ministers and members had been filled with Spirit since the outpouring at Camp Creek between 1896-1901.[54] Yet early in the twentieth century the church's pioneers were still focused on restoring the visible church based on a strict ethical discipline, rather than charismatic gifts. It was only after the outpouring of the Spirit during the great revival at Azusa Street in Los Angeles in 1906, led by C. F. Parham's former student from Houston, W. J. Seymour, that the church of God fully embraced the Pentecostal movement.[55] Tomlinson invited G. B. Cashwell, the "apostle of Pentecost in the South," who had been at Azusa Street, to preach the Pentecostal message at the General Assembly in 1908 in Cleveland.[56] Following his last sermon on January 12th, Tomlinson fell to the floor under the power of the Spirit. He professed to have spoken in at least ten different languages while in the ecstasy, and envisioned a world-wide harvest for the church through missionary outreach.[57] In the summer of 1908 he put up a tent in Cleveland and conducted a revival that swept the city. During the course of this crusade which lasted for several weeks, thousands attended, hundreds were saved, about 250 were baptized with the Spirit, and more than 150 joined the church.[58] Cleveland's *Journal and Banner* published that the religious fervor "is at white heat" and that the church had "captured all the east and north-east of Cleveland."[59] Sparks from this revival ignited other revivals in the surrounding towns and merged with the Pentecostal fires that were by then blazing throughout the Southeast.[60] Scores of evangelists joined the church between 1908-1910, finding freedom in the Pentecostal experience and haven in the church's government.

Nevertheless, the church's new Pentecostal identity met with strong opposition both from without and within the church. Local newspapers in Cleveland published articles that defamed the church and discredited the Pentecostal experience.[61] Within the church, the new assistant pastor at Cleveland, John B. Goins, and its prominent deacon, J. H. Simpson, contended against the doctrine of speaking in tongues as being the initial or primary evidence of Spirit-baptism, and amassed substantial support for their views.[62] They also charged that many manifestations attributed to the Spirit were fanatical and extreme. Goins' and Simpson's licenses were revoked and the Cleveland church excluded them, though Spurling seems to have disagreed with the action of the church against Simpson.[63] This contention resulted in a schism that rocked the Cleveland church between 1909-1910.[64] But the Pentecostal wave was by then too widespread and forceful to be abated by skepticism, ridicule, or theological contradiction. All resistance was soon overwhelmed; and thereafter the church of God was firmly established in the classical Pentecostal tradition. Nevertheless, some confusion over the "initial evidence" doctrine of Spirit-baptism was apparent even in 1911, when the subject was brought up in the General Assembly. After a sermon by Spurling and instructions by others, everyone "seemed to see eye to eye" that "some manifestations of the graces, gifts and fruits of the Spirit would evidence the abiding of the Spirit."[65] After further discussion on doctrine, this

Assembly adopted unamimously "Speaking in tongues as the evidence of the baptism with the Holy Ghost," and agreed that this teaching, with 24 others, should be published in *The Evening Light and Church of God Evangel,* and also in tract form.[66]

Time Line	Organizational Developments
1907	Name Church of God formally adopted
1910	*The Evening Light* and *Church of God Evangel* first published
1911	First children's home opened in Cleveland
1920	Centralized tithing system adopted by Assembly
1921	Constitution drafted, introduced and adopted by the Assembly
1922	Year of leadership problems and power struggle
1923	Power struggle ends in split. Tomlinson and followers start over having repudiated the Constitution of Council of Elders
1928	The year of "The Big Business Program"
1933	Church flag presented and approved by the Assembly
1939	Purchase of Bryant's home and initial work on Fields of the Wood
1941	Black field secretary appointed. First term of Bible Training Camp conducted
1943	Death of A. J. Tomlinson. Younger son M. A. Tomlinson selected to serve as General Overseer

The General Assembly

By 1905 a need was felt to hold an annual assembly to promote closer union and fellowship among the churches.[67] The first such meeting was held January 26-27, 1906 in the home of J. C. Murphy in Cherokee County, North Carolina. The next Assembly, held at Union Grove near Cleveland in 1907, formally adopted the name, Church of God.

The General Assembly of the churches marked a significant move toward centralized government. As early as the second Assembly in 1907 it was considered necessary for Spurling's 1886 credentials to be endorsed by the Assembly's officers.[68] F. J. Lee later considered the significance of the Assembly so important that he marked the church's beginning with the first Assembly in 1906.[69] Nevertheless, the authority of the Assembly and centralization were at first vehemently resisted, the Assembly being considered solely judicial in nature and purpose rather than executive or legislative. Fear of centralization was a legacy for the most part of the church's Baptist roots, with its idealism of local church independence and voluntary cooperation through associations and conventions. The history of persecution and tyranny in Europe's pope/king system of world government was still a vivid memory in the minds of church of God pioneers and, in fact, most Americans (particularly southerners) at the turn of the twentieth century. Indeed, the American state itself stood as a constant reminder of the grace and blessedness of religious and personal freedoms. Little by little, however, the General Assembly became authoritative and from it developed a hierarchy of episcopal authority over the churches. The General Assembly of the churches became the church's General Assembly. As centralization tightened between 1913-1922, some internal dissatisfaction emerged, for some held the church's original government and polity to be a sacred trust.[70]

Development of an Episcopal Hierarchy

The office of General Overseer grew out of the need for general leadership in the church, but also out of Tomlinson's perception of his own calling and sense of destiny.[71] Certainly his natural abilities and formal education made him head and shoulders above most of his friends and associates in southern Appalachia at the turn of the twentieth century.[72] He was considered outstanding even by men of the stature of Lemons and Lee. Moreover, the office was conceived when great pains were being taken to restore the church's apostolic government and ministry. The office of apostle was considered by many to be needful for the church's restoration, and thus many watched for signs in ministers that could identify them as last days apostles.[73] The Scriptures were thus searched and interpreted with those presuppositions in mind.[74]

In the 1909 General Assembly Tomlinson was selected to serve as the General Moderator of the Churches of God, with limited authority that included moderating the Assembly and licensing ministers. In 1910 the title of the position was changed to General Overseer and some further responsibilities added, which included the appointment of pastors. By 1912 Tomlinson began to see the office of General Overseer as being above the apostolic office, which he thought he found in James, the Lord's brother. He maintained that this particular James was not an apostle but above them in a solitary office that antityped Moses' position in Israel, and that filled Christ's place in the church on earth until He returned.[75] After he developed this interpretation and presented it to the General Assembly in his annual addresses in 1913 and 1914, it was accepted with enthusiastic support by most of the prominent ministers, including Lee and Lemons.[76] In the 1914 Assembly sentiments were expressed that lauded Tomlinson as being God's appointment for life.[77] Most everyone considered the office sacred with a special anointing and purpose. Tomlinson in particular maintained this opinion as long as he lived.[78]

After the office of General Overseer had been adopted in 1909, the need for a governmental position between the General Overseer and the churches became apparent. The need was met by the Assembly in 1911 and seven state overseers and an overseer for the Bahamas were appointed.[79] In 1913 the appointment of overseers became the responsibility of the General Overseer.[80] Thereafter, overseers were appointed as the church expanded in the states and territories at the General Overseer's discretion, and the state overseers began to make most of the pastoral appointments.[81] This established the basis for the general government of the church and its developing episcopal system.

Time Line	History of New Fields and Missions
1910	Mission Program started with visit to Nassau, Bahamas. Church established
1923	Jamaica
1926	Virgin Islands
1930	Missionaries to China
1931	Greece, Haiti, Canada East and West
1932	Costa Rica, Turks Island, Caicos Islands
1933	Manitoba, Saskatchewan
1934	Sierra Leone
1935	Barbados, Cuba, Egypt, Monserrat, Israel, Windward Islands
1937	British Colombia
1938	Alaska
1940	Dominican Republic, Hawaii, Puerto Rico
1943	Church established in 16 countries with 240 churches and 9,659 members

New Fields and Missions

The church's vision for restoration encompassed the world from the beginning. This was embodied at first in the idealism of Richard G. Spurling, whose vision had developed through his studies in church history and the missionary vision of nineteenth century Landmark Baptists. His prayer in 1897 revealed his vision as well as his burden:

> Oh, may some wise and noble one
> Complete the work we have begun,
> Oh, may it catch on every pen,
> And trace the isles from end to end.[82].

Nevertheless, Spurling was an idealist more than a man of action; and he lacked leadership ability and the kind of personal commitment needed to build a missionary organization. This development awaited the coming of A. J. Tomlinson, whose Christian experience had been planted and cultivated in a fervor of missionary activity in the late nineteenth century.[83] Perhaps no Pentecostal pioneer was better prepared to launch and sustain a missionary endeavor than Tomlinson. He had been educated at Westfield, Indiana's renowned Union Academy, hailed as one of the best schools in America in the 1880s.[84] After his conversion he attended the Bible and missionary schools of some of the most able men in America, including A. B. Simpson in New York, and Martin Wells Knapp, the founder of God's Bible School in Cincinnati.[85] Tomlinson was young, able, energetic, determined, educated, and equipped with organizational skills and a natural ability for leadership. Thus, the moment he joined the church in 1903 he set out to evangelize and plant churches.[86] After the Pentecostal message came to the Southeast from California in 1906, and took root particularly in North and South Carolina, Georgia, Alabama, Tennessee, and Florida by 1907, the Church of God simply rode the Pentecostal wave. Pentecostal pioneers such as G. B. Cashwell, F. M. Britton, M. M. Pinson, and J. H. King, blazed a trail through the Southeast opening the way for the planting of Church of God congregations. By 1909 Church of God ministers led by Tomlinson were in the forefront of the movement.[87] As the Spirit ignited revivals across the land, Church of God ministers were there to harvest the souls into local churches.[88]

Florida was particularly a hotbed of Pentecostal fervor. The annual South Florida Holiness campmeeting at Pleasant Grove near Durant was introduced to the Pentecostal movement in 1907 through the ministry of F. M. Britton.[89] This great meeting was opened to the Church of God in 1909 when Tomlinson was invited to be the campmeeting speaker through a special call of the Spirit.[90] The meeting was greatly blessed.[91] Pentecostal fire fell from heaven with all the manifestations of apostolic Christianity. Equally important, many of the people became convinced through Tomlinson's eloquence of the need for church order and discipline. Accordingly, 174 joined the Church of God before the meeting had closed, including many who had been stalwart opposers to organization.[92] Moreover, at least three bishops and deacons were ordained, and several evangelists were licensed, who returned home and brought several congregations into the church.[93]

This Florida campmeeting had attracted the attention of Edmond S. Barr and his wife, Rebecca, natives of the Bahama Islands. They were baptized in the Spirit in 1909, and greatly desired to return home with the Pentecostal message.[94] R. M. Evans (1847-1924), a Methodist minister, had been baptized in the Spirit evidently during F. M. Britton's meeting at Durant in July 1907. He later joined the Church of God, apparently during Tomlinson's meeting in 1909.[95] Evans also felt a definite call to go to the Bahamas, and made plans with the Barrs to evangelize the Islands. He helped fund the Barrs return home in November 1909, and later sold his home and livestock in order to provide passage for himself and his wife. Early in January 1910, the Evans' and Carl M. Padgett landed at Nassau, thus becoming the first missionaries representing the Church of God outside the United States. Tomlinson was excited about the venture and fully supported it.[96] He organized a Pentecostal band of musicians and preachers, and in the Spring of 1911 set sail with a party of 13 for the Bahamas to support and expand the work begun by the Barrs and Evans. The band remained in the Islands for several weeks establishing a front for the church's vision for world conquest. This venture marked the beginning of the church's world mission program.[97]

While this was happening in the Bahamas, other evangelists were being drawn into the church to help spread the holiness-

Pentecostal message. New contacts were made in Mississippi, Kentucky, Arkansas, and Virginia. Tomlinson himself had connections in most of the mid-West states; and Sam C. Perry visited Cuba laying the foundation for the future of the work there.[98] Miss Clyde Cotten, who had been instrumental in the great Cleveland revival, J. W. Buckalew, Efford Haynes, J. B. Ellis, H. L. Trim, M. S. Lemons, and others were dynamic evangelists with a vision to expand God's kingdom and to build the Church of God. Other men with gifts of administration and churchmanship, like F. J. Lee and T. L. Mclain, were rising to prominence in the developing government of the church. By 1911 all the ingredients were present to build a flourishing organization. In the next few years churches were organized in Maryland, Pennsylvania, Ohio, Michigan, Oklahoma, and Texas. Between 1911-1918 the church's membership grew nearly 500 percent, and doubled again by 1922. The Assembly statistics in 1922 showed 21,076 members, 666 churches, and almost 1000 ministers.[99]

Magnetic Attraction

By 1911 the name, "Church of God," was well on its way to becoming a household word in the South.[100] The zeal and unity of the ministers was magnetic; the church's order and government attractive; and Tomlinson himself was dynamic and charismatic, his personality seeming to command a following.[101] Moreover, it was the general sentiment among early Pentecostals that the "latter rain" had been poured out to break down denominational walls and barriers and to unite God's people in one body of Christ. These were some of the reasons that individual congregations and small groups were attracted to the church early in the twentieth century. It was the case with a small assembly of churches in northeast Tennessee and southeast Kentucky, going by the name, Church of God (now Church of God Mountain Assembly, Inc.). This group was centered in Jellico, Tennessee and was apparently contacted by J. B. Mitchell, J. S. Llewellyn, or Sam C. Perry.[102] In any case Tomlinson was invited to preach at their Assembly in 1911 and apparently made quite an impression.[103] Their assembly agreed to send chosen messengers to Cleveland for the church's Assembly in January 1912 with a view for organic union. Terms were drawn up and accepted by the Jellico delegation, amidst shouts of rejoicing by the assembly as the leaders embraced and gave to each other "the right hand of fellowship."[104] The Jellico messengers, however, were met at home with resistance and the union was never realized. Nevertheless, several of the ministers and members joined the church in the ensuing months.[105]

Church of God Evangel

The leaders of the church knew the value of the printed word. Tomlinson particularly was keenly aware of the value of a church paper. He had already experienced the benefits of a small paper, *Samson's Foxes* (1901-1902), in his mission work at Culberson. After he joined the church, M. S. Lemons assisted him at Culberson and later in Cleveland to publish *The Way* (1904-1905).

Between 1907 and 1910, G. B. Cashwell's paper, *The Bridegroom's Messenger*, published in Atlanta, became more or less the printed medium for Church of God ministers. In February 1908 Tomlinson became a corresponding editor, which made Church of God ministers feel at home with the paper. Tomlinson, W. F. Bryant, Jr., H. L. Trim, Flora Bowers, M. S. Lemons, and others all contributed reports and sermons to the paper. Funds were even solicited through the paper for missions and new field works to build the Church of God.[106] By 1910, however, the need for a paper to represent the peculiar needs of the church were pressing.[107] Thus the *Church of God Evangel* was launched on March 1, 1910, published its first year under the title *The Evening Light and Church of God Evangel*.[108]

Orphanage Work

At the turn of the twentieth century America still had not developed a social consciousness.[109] The tradition of rugged self-reliance remained the prevailing attitude and practice of "the land of the free and home of the brave." This democratic disposition intended to keep the federal government weak and out of the affairs of the people.[110] Consequently, there were few centralized support systems and federal welfare programs. Even public schools were slow in developing, especially on the frontier and in Appalachia. The responsibility of education most often fell upon the churches, or some community program supported by the churches. Care for orphans and widows also fell upon the compassion of the churches. This was considered the Lord's work, and the Lord's work was to be carried out by the church. Thus, Tomlinson and his good friend and co-worker, J. B. Mitchell, established an orphanage at Culberson shortly after they arrived in the mountains in 1899.[111] Tomlinson was inspired by George Mueller[112], the great orphanage builder in London, and otherwise was reared in the Quaker tradition, famous for building schools, orphanages, and doing benevolent work. It was thus almost inevitable that Tomlinson would encourage orphanage work after he became General Overseer, for it was considered at the heart of Christian service and befitting any church worthy of the name of Christ.

Not until 1911, however, was the first attempt made for a children's home. This work opened in Cleveland with 15 children under the supervision of W. F. Bryant, Jr. and two matrons. It was short lived, however, lacking funds and a leader who felt a special call and burden for this particular kind of work. In 1912, Mattie Perry, a female evangelist and the sister of Sam C. Perry, invited the church to visit her orphanage and school at Elhanan, North Carolina, near Marion. This meeting was scheduled with a view to merge the church and her Elhanan Institute.[113] The attempt failed apparently because Miss Perry felt the price for church government too high to surrender her independence.[114]

Finally, at the General Assembly in 1919 the Holy Spirit intervened during an address by the General Overseer and definite action was taken to commence a children's home.[115] The home was opened on December 17, 1920 under the matronship of Lillian Kinsey.[116] Thereafter, orphanage work became a permanent part of the church and continued in many countries after the need in the United States had diminished by the enactment of federal programs and stricter regulations.

Development of Doctrinal Distinctives

A formal body of doctrine was slow in developing in the church, for the impetus of the movement from the beginning had been on Christian unity, and doctrines were feared to be divisive and counter-productive toward that end, particularly when doctrines were formalized into a creed. Nevertheless, from the beginning the Missionary Baptist view of a general atonement was maintained over the more strict calvinistic view of a limited atonement, which in part occasioned the formation of Christian Union.[117] There was a simple *ordo salutis* of repentance, faith, and the new birth, which evidenced itself in obedience and suppression of carnal desires and self-indulgences.[118] Simple gospel standards were generally understood to be necessary to affirm the Christian profession. Thus, stealing, profanity, brawling, were all denounced, as well as polygamy and fornication.[119] Holiness in the first decade was apparently understood in terms of suppression rather than eradication.[120]

Spurling had outlined the basic conditions for the covenant of Christian Union "as it stood in 1895,"[121] which included the Lord's Supper, foot washing, and water baptism (though the mode of baptism had been debatable and thus Spurling tolerated sprinkling until the Assembly adopted "immersion" in 1911).[122] The New Testament was held to be "the only infallible rule of faith and practice" over against the legalisms of the law.[123] But love, and purity through love, were to be the ruling principles that undergirded everything in Christian Union.[124] These things made up the covenant by which Spurling endeavored to restore and formalize the visible church. All other matters were left to the individual's "christianized conscience" with the warning that "each member shall give an account to God for [himself]." [125]

This view began to change, however, after the church began to grow and Wesleyan and Pentecostal distinctives were acquired early in the twentieth century. Little by little doctrinal distinctives came to be considered important and even necessary to achieve Christian unity.[126] By 1902 entire sanctification became a part of the *ordo salutis*, and thus holiness standards became more strict. Divine healing was greatly emphasized after Tomlinson joined the church in 1903.[127] After 1908 Spirit-baptism evidenced by speaking in tongues was accepted (notwithstanding the Goins-Simpson dispute), and thereafter the church began to teach "signs following believers" and the full restoration of charismatic gifts.[128] Doctrines related to eschatology—heaven, hell, resurrection, and millenium—were discussed and generally agreed on before 1910. Strong drink and tobacco habits were denounced, though the use of tobacco was more or less tolerated until 1908[129]; and tithing in addition to offerings was considered biblical, though with some reluctance by Spurling and others (thus discipline was not to be imposed on those who did not tithe).[130] It was not until 1910, however, that a formal outline of all these teachings appeared in a definitive and codified form. They were first published in the *Evangel*.[131] There were 25 listed, including explanations that freed the church from dietary restrictions imposed under the law, and the observance of the Sabbath. In 1915 three teachings were added that imposed restrictions against "wearing of gold for ornament or decoration," "belonging to lodges," and "swearing."[132] These made a total of 28. Differences on the interpretation of "fornication" in Matthew 5:32 prevented "the divorce and remarriage question" from being settled conclusively. The door was left open for those considered to be victims ("innocent parties") of unfaithful companions and broken marriages; and this difference remained the "fly in the ointment" that prevented unity of opinion on the issue.[133] Between 1917-1920 the church taught "against going to war," but apparently the sober realities of World War I caused the church to rethink its position and by 1921 the doctrine had disappeared.[134]

Anatomy of a Disruption
Unit Two

Tomlinson's Autocracy

Once the position of General Overseer had been established and Tomlinson began to function acccording to its prescribed powers and responsibilities, some began to question the wisdom of granting so much authority to a single person. As early as 1913, mention had been made of dictatorial rule and lordship.[135] In 1915 Tomlinson apparently had been likened to a despot.[136] Talk began to circulate as to how the office might be held accountable and its vast array of powers limited. Some began to call for some type of counseling body to share the burden and responsibility of leadership in the church.

Council of Elders

In 1916 a resolution was adopted to create a twelve-man council to help guide and administrate the affairs of the growing organization and to hold in check Tomlinson's tendency to act unilaterally. The Council of Elders was formed by March of the next year.[137] Tomlinson endeavored to work with the Council but increasingly felt his autocratic style encroached upon.[138] Even from the outset he resented the method by which the members were appointed. The plan called for the General Overseer to appoint two of the Council members and the three together to appoint the remaining ten.[139]

Centralized Tithing System

A catalyst to the eventual disruption of the church was the revised financial system adopted by the Assembly in 1920. This system required all tithes from the local churches to be sent directly to world headquarters in Cleveland, where they would be distributed by a seven-man committee as the needs became apparent.[140] The system evidently was to work as a kind of Christian communism with a highly idealistic egalitarianism in view.[141]

In the following year, the General Overseer failed to comply with the Assembly's plan for a committee to oversee the finances, and rather took it upon himself to disburse the funds as he deemed wise and necessary.[142] This proved to be a grave mistake on Tomlinson's part, for as the needs were great everywhere and the funds limited, he was bound to be put in a bad light. Some of the pastors received little assistance from the tithe fund, while others received no tithes at all. Yet some others apparently received more than their share, or so it seemed.[143] As some fared better than others, Tomlinson seemed to be showing respect to persons and lording over the funds. The depression that was devastating the South at that time made the situation even more sensitive. Worse yet, Tomlinson used some of the tithes [$19,000] to help pay the debt on the newly built 4,000 seat Assembly auditorium and the *Evangel's* deficit, which by 1920 was nearly $23,000.00.[144] These unilateral decisions were unwise, to be sure, and gave occasion [when they were discovered] for doubts to be cast on Tomlinson's integrity and honesty.[145] Discontent began to mount over the management of the finances, particularly by some of the ministers in Cleveland.[146]

Over the next year the General Overseer continued to defend the centralized system in the *Evangel* and on the field.[147] But financial matters continued to worsen. Llewellyn apparently envied Tomlinson and desired to unseat him from the exalted office, and used the unfortunate circumstances to put the General Overseer in the worst light possible.[148]

J. L. Scott's Reformation

It was the move toward centralization that prompted J. L. Scott to reform with other dissidents in Chattanooga in 1919-1920. The name "The Original Church of God" expressed their intentions. They believed that the movement had been slipping off the rock of its original commitment and principles for several years, particularly in the move to centralize the local churches under an episcopal hierarchy headed by the General Overseer.[149] Added to this dissatisfaction was the growing sentiment among some leaders to make tithing compulsory and centralized.[150] To Scott and a small number of ministers in East Tennessee, Georgia, Kentucky, and Indiana, these were gross acts of apostasy that could not be tolerated. They declared independence and began their reform movement in Chattanooga, based more on Spurling's Landmark principles of equality and independence. Scott's move was encouraged after Sam C. Perry joined him in 1921.[151] Spurling himself also disagreed with the direction the church was taking, yet he remained with the organization (at least nominally) until matters grew worse in 1922.[152]

The Constitution

In the following months, matters grew worse in the struggle for power, and for what form of government the church should practice. Tomlinson continued to gain influence and prestige in the church, but certain other men had been increasing also in influence and stature among the people, namely, F. J. Lee, T. L. McLain (Lee's brother-in-law), J. B. Ellis, M. S. Lemons, and J. S. Llewellyn, all of whom sat on the Council of Twelve. Tomlinson's firm disposition about his exalted position irritated the relationship between himself and some of the Elders, to be sure, but Llewellyn was apparently a corrupt seed from the beginning. He had serious charges leveled against him in 1916 in his local church at Chandlers View, Tennessee, and was considered by many unfit to hold office as a bishop and especially to sit on the Council of Twelve.[153] Nevertheless, he had been appointed. Llewellyn thought in secular and business-like categories rather than pastoral and spiritual, and often confused church business with his own.[154] The confrontation was thus inevitable. Animosities were heightened when Tomlinson refused Llewellyn the use of the Evangel for promoting his personal interests.[155] This worked further ill-will between them, and occasioned a worse disposition in Llewellyn. Unscrupulously, he sowed discord and dissension, undermining and defaming Tomlinson. He eventually succeeded to draw J. B. Ellis, M. S. Lemons, W. F. Bryant Jr., and others into his scheme of things.[156]

Bryant was not on the Council of Elders but had been an influential and respected father in the church. He had been good friends with Tomlinson since the latter had arrived in the mountains in 1899, but had always resented his auto-cratic style of leadership.[157] Lemons had served with Tomlinson for 20 years in close Christian fraternity. He had come into the church shortly after Tomlinson in 1903, and with him had sacrificed and suffered privations and perse-cutions in order to build the church. Together with Bryant and J. B. Mitchell, and sometimes R. G. Spurling, they had walked for miles to pray for the sick, to distribute Christian literature and Bibles, and to preach the gospel. In 1904-05 they had worked together publishing *The Way*, and traveled together to Birmingham, Alabama in 1907 to seek for the baptism of the Spirit during M. M. Pinson's revival.[158] Tomlinson had even appointed Lemons as assistant General Overseer in 1913.[159] Nevertheless, Lemons was apparently poisoned by Llewellyn's venom, and joined in the movement to unseat Tomlinson, exemplifying on occasion an attitude that he doubtlessly regretted later.[160]

The seeds of dissension having been sown, they began to fester in the body of the church, particularly in Cleveland. Factions became more visible as the inward struggle contin-ued. Where Tomlinson refused to relinquish any of his power, others, led by Llewellyn, insisted on limitations. Some of the Elders were driven by the wrong spirit, to be sure, but they were also frustrated by Tomlinson's nearly totalitarian position. As the struggle continued, the nature of the situa-tion forced men to choose sides. Some of the more moderate and level-headed brethren waited at length until necessity drew them into the struggle. F. J. Lee had been supportive of Tomlinson's position, but eventually came to the conclusion that the office had to be accountable to someone besides God for the good of the church.[161] Lee thought the office was popish[162], and needed reformed so that its purpose and function was something "in" the church, not "over" it.

Some of the Elders reasoned with Tomlinson concerning his powers and responsibilities, and advised him of the dis-satisfaction that was mounting in Cleveland and on the field. Indeed some of these same leaders were agitating the dis-satisfaction.[163] Tomlinson proved more difficult than expect-ed, and refused to relinquish any of his powers believing that they were ordained by God. He considered the Elders to be merely his advisors, not his peers, and he insisted on retaining the final word on executive matters.[164] Ways began to be sought to circumvent Tomlinson's office. This opportunity came with the defection of J. L. Scott in 1919. Scott's success through the courts to obtain the church's property in Chattanooga and elsewhere was a perfect opportunity for Llewellyn to charge that the church's system was weak and inadequate.[165] His remedy was the Constitution, which he, Lee, and Lemons began to draft with Tomlinson's blessing. Tomlinson, being preoccupied throughout the year with the demands on his office in Cleveland and other responsibilities on the field,[166] had not thought through all the ramifications of the Constitution, presupposing that it was designed mainly to prevent a situation like Scott's from happening again. But in its preamble and eight articles revolutionary changes were made in the church's government and polity, which relieved some of General Overseer's responsibilities and unilateral powers. Ironically, Tomlinson himself introduced and endorsed the document in his annual address to the Assembly in 1921, and it was adopted.[167]

The following year Tomlinson saw his mistake in endorsing the Constitution.[168] The more its articles were implemented, the more he realized that it contradicted all that he had worked for in previous years, particularly in the establishment of his own position with its powers and privileges. Later, he denounced the Constitution as a creedal document and insisted that with it the church had completely apostatized. In the Called Council held in Chattanooga in 1923 he stated, "It was a creed that wrecked us in the year 1921 . . .", and a little later, "Since the passage of this Constitution we have not been the Church of God. . . . "[169]

In the 1922 Assembly Tomlinson met head-on with the Elders and the entire Assembly in calling for an abrogation of the Constitution. Moveover, he sought to gain back the little ground that he had given up in 1916 by having to share the responsibility of appointing ten of the Council's members.[170] Boldly he insisted for the practice to be amended so that he himself could unilaterally appoint the entire Council.[171] His annual address infuriated some of the leaders of the church, particularly Llewellyn, Lemons, J. B. Ellis, and others who had drafted the Constitution and served on the Committee for

Better Government. Tomlinson exalted his position as a "divine appointment" for life, insisting that it was totally out of the hands of man. He spoke of it "in high and ennobling terms," explaining on one occasion, "At times I was overwhelmed with awe because of the glimpses I got of the grandeur and sacredness of the new position." At the same time, he belittled the Constitution, speaking of "a puny little clause in our constitution,"[172] and charging that the Constitution had been the "direct cause of the trouble in the church."[173]

Thereafter the Committee was more determined than ever to maintain the Constitution, and also the established practice of selecting the Council of Elders. To add insult to injury, the Committee, led by Tomlinson's arch-antagonist, brought back to the Assembly a report that called for further limitations in the General Overseer's powers and a limited tenure of office.[174] Accordingly, the General Overseer would serve as one of a three-member Executive Council to oversee the church, including the appointment of the state overseers. Perhaps of more significance, the report recommended that the members of the Executive Council be selected annually.[175]

This report of the Committee on Better Government was unprecedented in the young organization, calling for sweeping reforms and directly confronting the autocratic style of Tomlinson. It sought to reverse what had been in the making since 1909—namely the office of General Overseer with its concomitant powers and responsibilities. But it also completely revolutionized the nature of the General Assembly, transforming it into an episcopal body.[176] The issues were forced on both sides. Tomlinson called the Assembly to prayer. Llewellyn thought it was a tactical move by Tomlinson to block the Committee's report, and, at that point, his true nature overtook him. While the Assembly was in prayer, Llewellyn rushed up to Tomlinson "in a rage and shook his fist and pointed his finger almost against [his] face and said, 'How dare you block this measure in any such way. You dare not do it, you shall not do it,' and walked away, white with madness."[177] After some objections to the proposed amendment, the Twelve Elders with the Seventy met in special session and passed the measure according to constitutional authority.[178]

The Final Break

The report on Better Government was too much for Tomlinson, who promptly elected for all or nothing. He tendered his resignation "to take effect as soon as his successors were installed."[179] But the Assembly refused it, hoping for matters to be resolved in better order—in peace and harmony. After several favorable comments in his behalf, Tomlinson reconsidered and agreed that evening to serve another year as General Overseer. Upon this decision, a tremendous response of approval—with manifestations of the Spirit—was made by hundreds in the Assembly. A large crowd lined up and for more than an hour passed by the platform to shake Tomlinson's hand and offer encouragement.[180]

But this was only an occasion for the moment—an emotional response primarily from the field. At headquarters—among the leaders—things were more divided than ever. Two opinions were set to prevail, one over against the other. Tomlinson's willingness to serve another year was only in hopes to rally a revolution to return the church to its former government under the exalted office he had filled since 1909. But there was little hope of this happening in a peaceful and orderly manner. For, first of all, Tomlinson's reputation had been badly damaged by Llewellyn and the "political wire-pulling" of those who were in league with him—but also by Tomlinson's own mistakes, which were many.[181] Secondly, the church had outgrown the autocratic style of Tomlinson. Mature and spiritual men, with high callings of their own, were no longer willing to submit to Tomlinson's exalted position.[182] On the other hand, many were disappointed with the behavior of some of the Elders, and with the measures that were passed in the Assembly [and the method by which they were passed].[183] Thirdly, and perhaps most importantly, Llewellyn was deeply enraged against Tomlinson; for he felt that Tomlinson had tricked him and the entire Assembly in the manner by which he had disclosed his errors.[184] In the Elders' Council held previous to the Assembly Tomlinson had been deeply sorrowful for his mistakes and showed a pentitent spirit before the Council.[185] He had wept deeply and asked for forgiveness and agreed to rectify the financial differences.[186] This was accepted apparently with weeping even on the part of Llewellyn.[187] But in the Assembly Tomlinson colored the whole affair in his favor. He made it seem that he had no choice in his decision in order to save the church from bankrupcy, and came out of his explanation appearing more as a hero than one who had abused his authority.[188] Thus the leadership of the church was deeply divided.

To make matters unbearable Llewellyn was selected as one of a three-man committee to investigate the apparent discrepancies in the various departments of the church.[189] The other two selected in the Elders' Council were F. J. Lee and J. B. Ellis.[190] The very nature of the work of the Investigation Committee was bound to grind on the situation, and Llewellyn's influence could do little more than speed up the approaching crisis. Tomlinson was uncooperative with the Committee. He was in principle offended by the affront of subordinates, and felt his integrity had been called in question; and perhaps he genuinely felt that submission to this Committee and/or the Elders' Council was wrong in consideration of his peculiar calling and exalted position. After all, these same men, with the exception of Llewellyn, had in 1914 themselves exalted Tomlinson and commended him for a life-time tenure in the office of General Overseer. In any case, Tomlinson was not disposed to work with a Committee that was now apparently "out to get him." Besides, he maintained that he was accountable only to God and the General Assembly.[191]

Moreover, Llewellyn had been selected by the Assembly in 1922 to serve as Editor and Publisher according to the new government provided in the amendment to the Constitution. This encouraged him all the more; he became bolder and more demanding. His position on the Executive Council in Cleveland while Tomlinson was on the field gave him a special advantage to effect his purposes.[192] The Committee ordered an audit of the books kept by Tomlinson after Llewellyn assumed office in December. When the "preliminary report" came back on April 12, 1923, it showed a shortage of $14,141.83.[193] Though the report was quite evidently incomplete and violated by Llewellyn's prejudices,[194] many with him "rushed to judgment" and word quickly circulated that Tomlinson was a crook. Nothing could have been further from the truth, but the seeds were sown to the wind and found fertile soil in suspicious minds. It was at this point that Lee clearly turned against Tomlinson, and fully sided with Llewellyn.[195] The die was now cast. The General Secretary, E. H. Boehmer, wrote Tomlinson several letters in New York, the Bahamas, and Florida, keeping him abreast of the developments in Cleveland. After the auditor's report, Boehmer became intimidated by Llewellyn and Ellis, and began to look out for his own interests, for it was becoming apparent how things were going to turn out for Tomlinson.[196] He urged Tomlinson to return home soon in order to have any chance of saving himself. Tomlinson remained in the South to fulfill his appointments, though heartsick and grieving in his spirit by the news and developing saga.

The differences grew more bitter and confrontational. Llewellyn and Ellis clearly wanted Tomlinson out of office, and by this time Lee and others thought the circumstances necessitated a change.[197] Slanderous accusations increased against Tomlinson; and finally Tomlinson allowed a counter-campaign to go against the antagonistic members of the Elders' Council, particularly Lemons, Llewellyn, and Ellis.[198] Contention and malicious gossip continued to disturb the peace of the saints. Rumors of "extortion," "wirepulling," "concussion," and other "chicanery"[199] flew over the church.

The Investigation Committee forged on, and so did Tomlinson. On June 12, 1923 the confrontation came to a head. The "June Council" convened in Cleveland with about 200 persons present, including the Council of Elders, the Council of Seventy and all ordained ministers who desired to attend. It is out of the scope of this short history to give minute details of the incidents as they transpired at that point; suffice it to say that Tomlinson and his two loyal followers on the Elders' Council, S. O. Gillaspie and George T. Brouayer, were overcome by the remaining ten elders.[200] Tomlinson was charged on 15 counts, including abuse of his office and authority, misappropriation of funds, and conspiracy against the church. He was subsequently impeached. Brouayer and Gillaspie were also impeached for "aiding and abetting Tomlinson in the principal part of his illegal acts," and for their disruptive conduct during the hearing.[201]

Tomlinson and his followers considered the proceedings of the "ten elders" to be mutinous and a travesty of justice, and subsequently met on June 27 and made a "Declaration" denouncing the Constitution and calling for a return to the

order of things before 1920.[202]   Later, considering the proceedings of the "ten elders" in the June Council to be illegal
[after Tomlinson had been relieved from the chair],
Tomlinson, Brouayer, and Gillaspie, met on July 24 for what
they considered to be a duly-called meeting of the Council.[203]
The "ten elders" did not attend and their offices were
declared vacant by the General Overseer and two "faithful"
elders present, Gillaspie and Brouayer. This seemed significant to them since the Supreme Judges—Court of Justice
had not yet ruled on the charges made by the "ten elders."

After the Supreme Court of Justice did rule in favor of the
"ten elders" faction on July 26,[204] Tomlinson and his followers denied the right and legality of all the proceedings, and
subsequently met in the home of H. A. Pressgrove in
Chattanooga to effect a total revolution of the church. In this
special Called Council held on August 8-10, 1923
Tomlinson was recognized as the God-appointed General
Overseer of the church and therefore moderated the meeting. The Constitution and the actions of the ten elders were
denounced and repudiated; and those present "[resolved
themselves back into being the Church]," and proceeded to
do business under the direction of the anointed General
Overseer without the Constitution or Council of Elders.[205]

Time Line	The "fight" for the name—Identity
1924	Legal action initiated over use of the name *Church of God*
1929	Further court action to clarify name complications
1933	First Business Guide published. It included an amended version of the covenant—the pledge of membership
1943	Development of Fields of the Wood. Church of Prophecy Marker Association established as an auxiliary. Increasing influence of Grady R. Kent
1951	Radio and recording ministry began
1952	Name Church of God of Prophecy agreed in the courts and was acceptable, finally settling the name dispute
1953	Hispanic field secretary appointed
1955	Tomlinson Memorial School established
1957	Resignation and revolt of Kent
1966	Founding of Tomlinson College

Tomlinson and His Followers

Unit Three

Starting Over

Tomlinson and his followers considered the actions taken in 1922-1923 to be bold but necessary steps to save the Church of God. The General Overseer was lauded for his courage and leadership, and thereafter was revered and followed with a sense of awe. Though fifty-eight years of age he was still full of energy and vision, and soon shook off any spirit of discouragement and proceeded with thrilling expectations of victories ahead.[206] He barely flinched at the accusations hurled against him and seemed to "count it all joy" to suffer for the Saviour and the cause he so much loved, namely, the Church of God. In the next few years he waded through court litigations, sometimes defying the decisions that he felt were unjust and an infringement upon his God-given conscience. He insisted on using the name, Church of God, after Bradley County's Chancery Court and Tennessee's Supreme Court ruled against him; and he was arrested and fined several times for his convictions.[207]

Shortly after the Called Council in Chattanooga Tomlinson returned to Cleveland and re-located across the tracks from his opposition and began to build a tabernacle for the up-coming Assembly in November.[208] Plans were made to begin publishing the church's new paper, *The White Wing Messenger*, which had been agreed upon in the Call Council in Chattanooga after a delegate claimed the Spirit had given him the name by special revelation.[209] In the Assembly that year official action was taken to abrogate the former Assembly resolutions that approved of the Constitution. In dramatic fashion Tomlinson glanced at his watch and instructed his secretary to take note: "At 4:30 P.M., November 23, 1923, the Assembly shook off the galling yoke of the Constitution and went free."[210]

And so Tomlinson was off again and running according to the vision that illuminated his way. He ignited passions for evangelism in his ministers and encouraged the sheep scattered during the disruption to return to the true fold.[211] By 1929 over fifteen hundred delegates registered in the Assembly and Tomlinson appointed overseers to twenty-six states and the Bahamas. "The reconstruction period," as Tomlinson called it (making a comparison to the American Civil War and Reconstruction Period)[212], was almost over. In 1928 he had devised a plan to more effectively harness the energies of the church and to cope with the depression that was then plaguing the South.[213] This was called "The Big Business Program"[214] and proved to be successful and beneficial, particularly for the support of the general leadership of the church and headquarters-sponsored programs. That same year Mr. and Mrs. J. B. Baney, Nell Thomas, and Lavenia Ferguson, deeded to the church the entire orphanage property at Dyersburg, Tennessee, valued at over fifty thousand dollars.[215]

Burger Mountain Tradition

Tomlinson had always given the Spurlings credit for "launching" the last-days church on August 19, 1886, which he had carefully recorded in his short history in **The Last Great Conflict**.[216] Following the disruptive period between 1919-1923, after Spurling, Bryant, J. L. Scott, Sam C. Perry, and others had parted ways with him and with each other, he gradually began to change his view.[217] He noted in his annual address in 1929, "Those who started with me, and whom I believed to be ahead of me in the search, well where are they now? But I drop the curtain and pass on."[218] Thereafter he began to date the church's restoration with his personal experience on Burger Mountain on June 13, 1903.[219] His son, Homer, son-in-law, A. D. Evans, and Grady R. Kent embellished and mythologized the event until Tomlinson was gradually perceived as "the first member of the church this side of the Dark Ages."[220] This interpretation became canonized and was regarded by the next generation as a sacred and inviolable tradition.[221]

Fields of the Wood

The June 13th tradition was enhanced in 1939 when Tomlinson revisited the place where Bryant's cabin stood at the base of Burger Mountain, and thereafter decided to purchase the property in order to memorialize the event.[222] Grady R. Kent's message in 1940 referring to Tomlinson's experience on Burger Mountain as the fulfillment of Psalm 132:6 and other passages further solidified Tomlinson's sentiment and occasioned the name of the memorial to be called Fields of the Wood.[223] Homer further mythologized the event by drawing a parallel between his father's Burger Mountain experience and Moses' experience on Mount Sinai.[224] Tomlinson became preoccupied in his last years with the project, spending much of his time planning and starting the work on the project.[225]

The Prophetic Ensign

After the major division in 1923 Tomlinson began to contemplate the need to adopt an ensign to distinguish the church from the "elders' faction" and other religious bodies.[226] Understanding the church in the image of a political nation reinforced the idea of a flag to represent God's "holy nation."[227] Scriptural references to flags, banners, and ensigns began to be seen as prophetic and needed only to be brought to material fruition and fulfillment.[228] After a message by O. S. Carter during West Virginia's convention in 1933 affirmed Tomlinson's impulse, plans were made to develop a design.[229] The flag was presented to the General Assembly in 1933 and, after several emotional outbursts and messages in tongues and interpretations, the flag was considered approved by the Holy Spirit;[230] and thereafter was considered the fulfillment of Psalm 60:4.

The flag—representing "the great Church of God"—was believed to be a rallying standard through which God would unify all Christians in "one fold" in answer to Jesus' prayer and teachings in John 10,17. Thus the refrain from a favorite Church song,

> Come under the ensign of God,
> Come now and unite in the fold.
> The standard of the great Church of God,
> The ensign will wave as we go.[231]

The symbol of the flag deepened the church's sense of peculiarity and exclusiveness.[232] Thousands were manufactured and displayed in churches and homes, and flag stickers were made for display in automobiles.[233] Tomlinson's enthusiasm for the flag, and his unfortunate choice of phrases to describe it on occasion,[234] apparently led some to make an icon of the symbol. This caused some embarrassment and occasioned the church to be held in derision by its critics.[235] The tendency to elevate the flag beyond its symbolic purpose prompted Assembly resolutions to correct abuses and irregularities.[236]

A Banner Year

In 1936 the church reached a zenith of anticipation when Francisco Olazabal, a dynamic Mexican minister, joined the church. Olazabal was the administrative head of a body of churches that totaled approximately fifty thousand members.[237] Homer had become close friends with Olazabal after the "Great Aztec" had moved to Queens, New York near where Homer had established the church's state office.[238] There Olazabal had built a substantial following, drawing city-wide attention through miraculous healing services. Homer convinced Olazabal to unite with the church, and staged the ceremony to take place at the Assembly in 1936.[239] Olazabal was invited also to conduct the annual healing service during the Assembly [which Homer had been in charge of for several years].[240] Great fair was made of the event, including Olazabal's union with the church and the expectation of thousands of new members. The story was carried by Cleveland, Chattanooga, and New York newspapers, and spread nationwide via the Associated Press. This created great anticipation in the church, which Homer [who was serving as General Secretary of Foreign Languages as well as State Overseer of New York] cultivated into a vision for world evangelism.[241] Olazabal met an untimely death in a car accident the following year traveling with his wife through Texas.[242] This had an adverse effect immediately on the Latin work, and the union with Olazabal's followers was never fully realized; but an appetite for world evangelism had been created in the church which did not go away.

"The Great Speckled Bird"

The great interest in world missions joined with the church's deepening exclusiveness in the early 1940s, and prompted the church's leaders to employ the motif of the "Great Speckled Bird."[243] Misunderstanding Jeremiah 12:9, which depicts God's judgment against Israel's transgressions, the passage was used rather to support the church's mission to all races. Thus the "speckled bird" represented ethnic diversity rather than sins.[244]

However, the motif was not original with the Church of God. The lyrics were first composed apparently by a "Reverend Gant" and later set to music borrowing the melody from A. P. Carter's love song, "I'm thinking tonight of my blue eyes."[245] In 1937 Reverend Guy Smith claimed authorship and had it published by M. M. Cole Publishing Company in Chicago.[246] It was popularized in the late 1930s after Roy Acuff performed it at the Grand Ole Opry in Nashville. It was received with such delight that he was requested to do three encores.[247] Somehow Homer Tomlinson acquired the copyright to the song in 1941 and adapted it for the Church of God as if it had been especially prepared for it.[248] The motif was celebrated and remained popular in the church until the early 1980s.[249]

Minorities

Tomlinson had always been open to interracial worship and fellowship, due probably to his Quaker background and education.[250] But as the church was centered and concentrated in the South, the full expression of his openness in this regard was suppressed. Nevertheless, the church was probably the first to defy Jim Crow laws.[251] In 1941 Tomlinson appointed a black field secretary, Ralph C. Scotton, to assist the office of General Overseer.[252] This became a powerful position that opened the way for black leadership in the church.

Likewise, Tomlinson readily employed the use of women in the ministry, appointing them to pastorates as well as international positions, but forbidding them ordination and participation in the business affairs of the church, based on certain passages that were interpreted to indicate the distinctive role of men as heads of their homes and elders in the church.[253]

Bible Training Camp

Bible Training Camp was recommended in 1939, but its first term was not realized until August 4-31, 1941 with 42 students.[254] It was designed to establish and train ministers in the doctrines and practices of the church, and to prepare them for full-time service in the church.[255] Being held in Cleveland with several of the teachers serving also under general appointment added prestige to the Bible camp. The new institution was received with such enthusiasm throughout the church that by the third term, April 4-30, 1943, over two hundred students enrolled from twenty states and four countries.[256] Bible Training Camp was destined for a prominent place in the church's future.

Time Line	Continuing International Growth
1944	Central America, Mexico
1946	Panama
1949	Aruba, Saint Kitts
1950	Antigua
1951	Anguilla, Guatemala, Leeward Islands
1952	England, Honduras, Philippines
1954	Bermuda, El Salvador, Nevis, Philippines, Sweden, Trinidad/Tobago
1955	Argentina, Peru, Bermuda
1956	Australia, British Guyana
1957	Uruguay, India
1958	Saint Vincent
1959	Holland, Switzerland, St. Lucia, Germany
1961	Turkey
1962	St. Martins, Nicaragua
1963	Barbuda
1964	Grenada
1965	Brazil, Cyprus, Botswana
1967	South Africa
1968	Thailand, Venezuela
1969	Korea
1971	Indonesia, Nigeria
1973	Colombia
1974-1975	Bolivia, Chili

The church was now established in 48 countries, with 1,784 churches, and more than 100,000 members in these countries.

A Great Warrior Laid to Rest

After many difficult battles, and a faithful enlistment for his Master, A. J. Tomlinson was laid to rest in the city that he proclaimed to be "The capitol of the world for the Church of God."[257] He had been a living legend since 1923, and grew to "bigger than life" before he passed over the tide on October 2, 1943.[258] He was loved deeply and revered by thousands. His exploits were legendary, the stuff from which myths are made, and so they were. He left a legacy among his followers that was rich but not infallible. A sentiment expressed in his last annual address—"I see nothing but victories on top of victories [for the Church of God]"—and his last entry in his celebrated diary—"Great things close by now"—were embraced as prophetic expectations by the next generation of the church.[259]

Defection of Homer A. Tomlinson

The death of A. J. Tomlinson in 1943 left a huge void in the church for leadership: for the church had been structured to depend on the office of General Overseer for direction since 1909. Tomlinson's eldest son, Homer, presupposed that he was in line for the position, based in part on his interpretation of some of his father's comments. He referred in particular to an article in the April 18, 1942 issue of the *White Wing Messenger*.[260] After all, he alone had been witness to his father's work since 1899 in the mission at Culberson. And since the revolution in 1923 he had committed himself to his father's ministry and vision for the Church of God.[261] Moreover, he had prepared himself with a formal education at the University of Tennessee and was experienced as a state overseer, general secretary of foreign languages, and pastor; and he was a gifted writer.[262] Nevertheless, many of the presbyters were uncomfortable with some of his strange ideas and business tactics, and during their meeting to select an interim General Overseer, chose Milton A. Tomlinson, his younger brother, after a message in tongues was interpreted to say, "Bring forth thy younger son."[263]

After having at first approved of his brother's selection, Homer soon became dissatisfied with the decision, and struck out on his own on December 9, 1943 with a small group of followers, mainly in New York where he had been Overseer for several years.[264] He named his faction, The Church of God, which became little more than a support group for his colorful but bazaar campaigns to become President of the United States and King of the World![265]

New General Overseer

After being installed in the exalted position of General Overseer on October 7, 1943, Milton A. Tomlinson (1906-1995) immediately set out to fill the agenda set by his father, for this was the counsel of his advisors and expectation of the church in general.[266] He took his cue for the next generation from the Burger Mountain tradition and focused a great deal of his attention on the Church of Prophecy Marker Association, particularly on Fields of the Wood, leaning heavily on the vision of Grady R. Kent, whom his father had magnified before he died.[267] He also gave considerable attention to the further development of Bible Training Camp. It soon became the official teaching arm of the church and continued to gain prestige under the supervision of L. A. Moxley, A. D. Evans (Milton's brother-in-law), and later J. B. Wright.[268]

Idealism of the General Assembly

Since 1906 the tradition of the General Assembly had grown year after year into a sacred institution. Tomlinson praised the Assembly continually as "the most noble body on earth," and often compared it to the American political system of government.[269] He patterned many of its features after national political conventions, including the names of certain committees and the pageantry of state marches and flag waving.[270]

After the so-called "civil war" in 1923 he continued to elevate the ideal of the Assembly, referring often in his annual addresses to its origin in Acts 15 and its restoration beginning in 1906.[271] This left the impression that the Acts 15 council was an institution (if not annual) and current Assembly practices were often juxtaposed beside or transposed over it, so that the Acts 15 council was interpreted by current Assembly thinking rather than vice-versa. In any case, Tomlinson's descriptions of the nature and purpose of the Assembly created a sense of awe in the church for the annual event and correspondingly for its anointed "chief executive."[272]

Proverbs 11:14—"Where no counsel is, the people fall: but in the multitude of counsellors there is safety"—became a well-known and often quoted passage in the church; but the intention of the writer was exaggerated and this occasioned a sense of infallibility to be attached to the General Assembly. Thus when the first Business Guide was published in 1933 by A. D. Evans, Tomlinson's son-in-law, it altered the original covenantal pledge for church membership to include absolute loyalty to the General Assembly:

"Will you sincerely promise in the presence of God and these witnesses, that you will accept this Bible as the Word of God—believe and practice its teachings as interpreted by the General Assembly—the New Testament as your rule of faith and practice, government, and discipline, and walk in the light to the best of your knowledge and ability—will you pay tithes into the church and practice all other activities as instructed by the General Assembly?" The obligation required the applicant to answer—"I will."[273]

The Business Guide added a special note to this covenant formula: "Loyalty to the General Assembly, is one of the chief principals [sic] to be emphasized, but this is only being loyal to the Bible because the General Assembly of the Church of God stands for the whole Bible rightly divided. This includes helps and governments."[274] This idealism of the General Assembly became entrenched through the church's official teaching arm, Bible Training Camp.

Back into the Courts

Milton had fallen heir to the long and expensive litigation for the right to use the name, Church of God. The legal action had been initiated in February 1924 by Llewellyn, Lee, and Lemons, in behalf of their faction of the broken body. After contradictory rulings in the lower courts, the Supreme Court of Tennessee finally ruled in favor of the Llewellyn-Lee faction and ordered Tomlinson and his followers to use "Tomlinson" as a prefix to the name Church of God, to distinguish the factions.[275] This was considered final, but was unacceptable to Tomlinson's followers on the field, for the name, Church of God, had become sacred to them.[276] An array of protest was raised, and in 1929 the court offered some relief for the defendant group, allowing for a qualifying suffix instead of the Tomlinson prefix. Thereafter, the church went by the name, "Church of God, over which A. J. Tomlinson is General Overseer."[277] But this was not acceptable to the complainants, who further complained in the ensuing years that business matters and money were still being confused. They were particularly agitated by road signs erected in Cleveland that advertized "Welcome to Cleveland: World Capitol for the Church of God," with the address of the general offices of Tomlinson and his followers. Thus an injunction brought "Case Number 1891" back into court on May 1, 1952.[278] Chancellor Glen W. Woodlee ruled that the church could use the name, Church of God of Prophecy, rather than Tomlinson Church of God, but one or the other had to be used for the court's patience was exhausted.[279] The name, Church of God of Prophecy, was acceptable, for A. J. Tomlinson and others had referred often to the church as the "church of prophecy."[280] Finally, after twenty-eight years the matter was settled.

But not for Homer Tomlinson. Milton's "thorn" since 1943 seized the opportunity for publicity. In his typical zany fashion, he traveled to Cleveland, went through the motions of relieving Milton as General Overseer, and filed for a suit to obtain the church's properties around the world.[281] Homer then traveled to Fields of the Wood, after he had notified the local newspaper and sheriff's department, and, carrying a sledge hammer, climbed Ten Commandment Mountain and proceeded to break up the large concrete letters of the Eighth Commandment.[282] According to his plan he was jailed in Murphy, North Carolina near Fields of the Wood[283], vainly imagining that his antics would gain some sympathy for his lost cause.

Defection of Grady R. Kent

Since the 1930s Kent (1909-1964) had been rising to some prominence, serving as overseer of the churches in Vermont, Minnesota, and Nebraska between 1934-1938.[284] In 1938 he moved back to Georgia, his home state, and began pastoring at Egan.[285] There he gained considerable attention during a trial over a severe beating that he had received from the whips of Ku Klux Klansmen.[286] The trial was highly publicized particularly by the attendance of Georgia's governor, Gene Talmadge.[287] Tomlinson had also attended, and following the verdict which brought the Klan to justice, Tomlinson decided to appoint Kent to the pastorate at Cleveland.[288] Though lacking formal education, Kent had a charismatic personality that made him likeable and enabled him to find favor in the church, particularly with A. J. Tomlinson. He came into further favor with Tomlinson after preaching the message in 1940 (mentioned above) that depicted Tomlinson's 1903 experience on Burger Mountain as the fulfillment of prophecy.[289] This resulted in the development of Fields of the Wood and a new auxiliary in the church named the Church of Prophecy Marker Association.[290] Kent was appointed to oversee the work in 1943[291] and continued to gain popularity, while expanding the ministry of the association through new projects. He was extremely imaginative and exciting to a large element of the church's constituency, preaching sometimes for three and four hours on prophetic and apocalyptic themes. One of his spectacular projects was the development of the White Angel Fleet, an airforce of over 100 single engine prop planes, that he depicted as fulfilling prophecy.[292] "Ezekiel's Cherubim," as he called them, put on shows at various airports in order "to gain the attention of the world for the church."[293] "The church" became his overarching theme which he romanticized as "The Woman of Prophecy."[294] This extravagant and lofty view of the church further pushed the organization in the direction it was already leaning.

By 1950 Kent was extremely popular but had come into conflict with the Bible School's powerful superintendent, J. B. Wright. The two leaders, worlds apart in opinion and personality, represented a growing dichotomy in the church that had been developing since 1948, after a resolution had passed in the General Assembly that made the General Overseer subject to the General Assembly.[295] Kent disagreed with the decision, and ever after felt that he was filling a void in theocratic government that Milton A. Tomlinson created when he submitted to the Assembly's decision.[296]

Kent's apocalyptic imaginations began to overwhelm his better judgment in the early 1950s. He began to see himself as the fulfillment of one of the two witnesses in Revelation 11, and by 1955 was boldly declaring himself to be John the Revelator. Kent's claims were denounced by the General Assembly in 1956[297] and, after he persisted in his claims, was called to account by the General Overseer.[298] He resigned his ministry under Tomlinson and proceeded to lead a revolt with his followers on February 13, 1957, which he likened to Tomlinson's revolt in 1923 to save the church from apostasy.[299] He interpreted the action as the fulfillment of Zechariah 13:8-9 and used (or misused) other passages to designate it the "second Reformation" of the last days Church of God. He named his defecting group of churches, The Church of God of All Nations [later The Church of God], and declared himself to be the chief bishop. It was estimated that by 1958 about 800 members had defected with him.[300]

Time Line	Further Internationalization of the Church
1976	South Africa/B—Afrik., Portugal, Zimbabwe
1977	Ghana, Malawi, Paraguay, Swaziland, Zambia
1978	Ivory Coast, Cayman Island, Kenya, Tanzania
1979	Liberia, Mozambique, Democratic Rep. of Congo (former Zaire)
1980	Belize
1981	Finland, Samoas, Spain, Uganda
1982	Ecuador, Japan, Rwanda
1983	Belgium, Malaysia, Singapore
1985	Benin, France, Guadeloupe
1986	Martinique
1987	Burkina Faso
1991	Togo, Pakistan, French Guyana, Bulgaria
1992	Suriname
1994	New Zealand., Figi
1995	Kazakhstan
1996	Namibia, Romania, Italy, Ethiopia, Byelorussia

Church established in 104 countries with 4,152 churches and 278,221 members.

Milton Comes Into His Own

Unit Five

A Skillful Manager

Through all the difficulties with Homer, Kent, court litigations, and the everyday burdens of the office, Milton forged on and gained respect for his fortitude and steadfastness. Though lacking in personal gifts he developed skills that enabled him to manage the church. He had the ability to recognize gifted men and women and allowed them to rise to prominence to share in the leadership of the church. He became a skillful chairman, acting on suggestions that he perceived could advance the work of the church. He learned to be cautious and deliberate, and, unlike King Rehoboam, wisely listened to and respected the experienced elders in the church.[301]

Ministries were expanded and diversified during his tenure. In 1951 the church entered radio and developed a recording ministry. This led in 1970 to the celebrated Voice of Salvation broadcast (translated in four languages). In 1953 he appointed an Hispanic field secretary, J. A. Jimenez, to assist with the growing works in Latin America and the Spanish-speaking churches in the United States. In 1970 the evangelism department was created and in 1971 the Voice of Salvation began to be televised, overcoming earlier Assembly resolutions that forbade members to own televisions.[302] Subscriptions to the *White Wing Messenger* exceeded 20,000 by 1987, and were published in eight languages.

Thus, after living in the shadow of his illustrious father for more than fifty years, Milton came into his own. The acute sensitivity to what "papa had said" or what "the former General Overseer had envisioned" was gradually eclipsed by his own work and vision. Perhaps because Milton was not as gifted as his father he developed skills that made him a superior administrator, learning to employ the gifts of other

61

men that together excelled his father's. Perhaps his personality, less eccentric and complex than his father's, proved to be in the long run a more stabilizing and consistent influence in the church. Perhaps a genuine sense of humility made him realize his own limitations and depend more on God. Certainly his longevity in office was a factor that contributed to the develpment of his own identity. By the 1960s a new generation was coming on that knew only the exalted office of General Overseer in the person of Milton Tomlinson. A. J. Tomlinson [born in 1865] was becoming more and more a figure of the distant past.[303] In any case, the progress of the church under Milton's leadership was phenomenal, especially in consideration of the social strata of the majority of its members. Upon his resignation in 1990 official reports showed over 260,052 members and 5,357 churches in 91 countries.[304]

Emphasis on Education

The absence of any emphasis on higher education had been noticeably missing in the church between 1923-1958. This was occasioned by the disruption in 1923, which had been blamed in part on the arrogance of educated men. Tomlinson explained in the Called Council in 1923 "Too much stress no doubt has been laid on education. And because some have not much education is no reason God is not with them, or that they have no wisdom. If you . . . have felt cramped because you lack education I want you to get out of it and feel free."[305] Later that year in his address to the General Assembly, he said, "There has been a spirit working among us for years that has been making a gap between the educated and those who have been deprived of educational advantages. This spirit has the tendency to crush down the uneducated and prevent their having anything to say in the Assembly. I have battled this spirit all these years, and now I am going to come out boldly and declare myself for the common people."[306]

While Tomlinson meant well, thereafter an anti-intellectual disposition permeated the church. Formal education was generally considered dangerous or else a waste of time and money that could be better spent on evangelism and building the church. Bible Training Camp was hardly worthy of the name of education, since students were not taught to think for themselves but to parrot established doctrine and practices.[307] This actually stifled intellectual development and more or less rubber-stamped the next generation of leaders.

Some rethinking about formal education began to take place in the early 1950s, which led to the establishment of Tomlinson Memorial School in 1955. Organized with elementary [grades 1-8] and secondary [grades 9-12] divisions, the school endeavored to reconcile spiritual experience and the Bible with science, math, literature, English, social studies, and business.[308] This led to the founding of Tomlinson College in 1966, offering two-year degrees in ministry and liberal arts disciplines. The infant institution struggled from the outset since the church had not emphasized higher education for more than forty years. But the General Overseer was behind it, and so it survived. The appearance of the college campus was impressive, developed on the beautiful 100 acre tract of land in north Cleveland that was purchased in 1945 to serve the orphanage work.[309] Though gaining full accreditation in 1983, and developing a four-year degree program in Bible in 1989, the college never gained enthusiastic support in the church, and continued to be underwritten substantially by the church's general funds.[310]

Smooth Sailing

After Kent's defection in 1957 the church was at peace, and for the most part a state of euphoria permeated the entire organization for the next three decades. Milton Tomlinson had become well established behind the helm, and generally the church enjoyed smooth sailing (notwithstanding the defection of a minister now and then, and the tragic death in 1976 of Harry Lee Moore, one of the most outstanding ministers in the church).[311]

A Vision Fulfilled

After a fire destroyed the publishing house in February 1967, the church purchased forty-one acres of prime property about two miles south of the Tomlinson College campus on the north side of Cleveland, anticipating the development of a modern headquarters' complex.[312] This began to be realized in 1968 with the construction of a publishing house encompassing 50,000 sq. ft. of floor space, including modern offices, bookstore, and the latest printing equipment. In 1970 an additional acre was purchased with a building that was remodeled to facilitate a communications' center for radio and television ministries.[313] This was followed in 1972 with the construction of an impressive Assembly tabernacle that seated over 10,000.[314] And in 1975 the ultra modern international office building was completed, with almost 60,000 sq. ft. of office space on three levels.[315] Upon completion of this impressive complex Milton considered his labor for the Master near completion.[316]

End of an Era

Though still determined in spirit, Milton's physical strength had been diminishing according to nature for several years, and finally got the best of him following the Assembly in September 1989. He quietly began to make plans to resign and made the announcement public in February of the next year. The presbytery of the church gathered for a special called meeting and selected Billy D. Murray, Sr. on May 2, 1990 to be the interim General Overseer until the up-coming Assembly.[317] The presbytery's selection was accepted by the Assembly on August 13, 1990 without a dissenting voice.[318] This was rather amazing for some were bitter against him.[319] Thereupon, Murray recognized Milton's long and faithful service to the church and arranged for him to be honored with the title of General Overseer emeritus[320], which he retained until he died on April 26, 1995.[321] Milton's 46 years and 7 months in office as General Overseer remains the second longest tenure by a chief executive officer in Pentecostal history, second only to C. H. Mason of the Church of God in Christ. Back to back, Milton and his father served the office of General Overseer for 80 years,[322] and their lives spanned almost the entire history of the holiness-Pentecostal movement in the nineteenth and twentieth centuries.[323]

Time Line	"The Paradigm Shift"
1975	International Office building completed
1983	M. A. Tomlinson served for forty years
1990	Failing health forces Tomlinson to resign. Billy D. Murray selected to serve as interim General Overseer. Committee appointed to study the office of General Overseer
1991	Murray confirmed as General Overseer by the Assembly. Financial investment failure
1992	General Assembly moved to Louisville, Kentucky, and becomes a two-year event. Tomlinson College closed, Bible Training Institute suspended
1993	"Concerned Group" forms separate organization
1994	**"Turning to the Harvest"** paradigm. A critical General Assembly where new Assembly business procedures were adopted, and the "plurality of leadership" starting with at least two presbyters to work with the General Overseer was accepted. Radical changes to the church's financial system proposed but held over for further work
1995	Death of M. A. Tomlinson
1996	Restructuring of International Offices announced along with the appointment of Ministry Directors to replace departments and auxiliaries leaders. Role of women clarified and an increased level of ministry responsibility and involvement accepted by the General Assembly. Finance and Stewardship report accepted
1997	Selection of General Presbyters
1998	Murray announces resignation

In 1990 when Murray became General Overseer, the membership in the nations was reported as 194,146. Today the membership in the nations is 344,501. Membership in North America has remained steady between 70-75,000. Worldwide membership has increased by more than 60% since Murray became overseer.

A Stormy Transition

Unit Six

Critical Period

Murray assumed the office of General Overseer at a critical period in the church's history. For years issues had been seething in the body of the church. Since 1983 Tomlinson at 76 years of age, and in his fortieth year in office, felt that his calling had been fulfilled according to a traditional view that the office of General Overseer had been ordained for forty years.[324] But as things happened God did not intervene otherwise and Milton continued in office. Thereafter his policy was more or less to maintain the *status quo* of traditional practices and to avoid new and pressing issues. Year after year issues were skirted and Assembly agendas were prescribed to avoid as much as possible debates and new judications.[325] And when issues were argued on the Assembly floor, they were often cut short and "tabled."[326] This had caused strong undercurrents to develop in the church, and when Tomlinson announced his resignation in 1990 the situation was explosive on several fronts.[327] Though still offering a healthy and vibrant appearance on the outside, the church was deeply troubled internally.

The choice of Murray itself was problematic, for he represented a progressive element in the church that longed for outdated and out-moded traditions to be laid aside so that the church could "get on with" its divine commission. His messages were one of the biggest attractions in the Assemblies throughout the 1980s and were always powerful and challenging, but, by the nature of the circumstances, tended to distance those with traditional mind-sets. Thus, when he was selected as General Overseer he was met with strong resentment on the part of some, though he had an impeccable record of service and loyalty in the church for over 45 years.[328]

tended to distance those with traditional mind-sets. Thus, when he was selected as General Overseer he was met with strong resentment on the part of some, though he had an impeccable record of service and loyalty in the church for over 45 years.[328]

Murray endeavored to reconcile differences and, at the same time, remain faithful to his vision for the church. But the kinds of changes that circumstances demanded were bound to confuse a great many, and negative situations were magnified by those who were already resentful. Whatever the new General Overseer did was bound to displease one faction or the other, for the church was inwardly divided. The die seemed to be cast. Murray decided to go with his best judgment, being encouraged by the overwhelming majority of the church that selected him, while the dissenters grew more disgruntled.[329]

Tomlinson College Closed

One of the church's greatest financial liabilities was Tomlinson College. For years it had been underwritten by general funds averaging nearly $500,000 per year. After several avenues were probed to find a solution, it was finally concluded that the church's budget could not carry the burden.[330] The decision laid with the General Overseer and Administrative Committee, not the Assembly. And so the college was closed on May 24, 1992.[331] It was a sad day in the church. The difficult and unpopular decision nearly devastated some of the faculty and sent more shock waves vibrating through the church.[332]

A Painful Schism

While the new administration was preoccupied with seeking solutions for the financial crisis at General Headquarters, a doctrinal issue was simultaneously capturing the attention of the church on the field. The church's teaching on outward adornment had been blamed for years for stunting the growth of the church. Traditionalists, however, maintained that the teaching was consistent with holiness standards and the doctrine of the apostles, particularly citing traditional references in 1 Timothy 2:9 and 1 Peter 3:3.[333]

The issue eventually boiled down to the wedding band.[334] Some maintained that the wedding band was a pagan tradition while the majority of the church felt that it was a worthy symbol of marriage and that it encouraged fidelity.[335] The issue dominated the 1991 Assembly, and was settled only after a substantial number reluctantly submitted to the majority of the delegation.[336] But it was not a happy submission. Many that submitted had already developed an interchurch identity that had come to be known as "The Concerned Group."[337] Their basic "concerns" were over talk that suggested changes or modifications in the church's "twenty-nine prominent teachings" to which they were committed in order to maintain the *status quo*. But they were equally committed to Tomlinson's 1939 revision of the church's history relative to his experience on Burger Mountain in 1903.[338] The Burger Mountain tradition informed their interpretation of the nature and process of "theocratic government" and the exclusive status of the Church of God of Prophecy.[339] Some of the ministers from this group met separately and filed a lawsuit against the Administrative Committee over the misfortunate investment with Custom Trading International Corporation.[340] This necessitated disciplinary action by the Presbytery which, after pleadings and counseling to no avail, resulted in the revocation of several of their licenses.[341] Most of these ministers with others in "The Concerned Group" proceeded to "draw away disciples" and subsequently formed a separate organization in the Summer of 1993.[342] They chose Robert J. Pruitt (who had encouraged the lawsuit and schism)[343] to be their General Overseer and, like Homer Tomlinson's and Grady R. Kent's groups before them, claimed to be the continuation of the original church and adopted the name, "The Church of God."[344]

When all was said and done, only about one percent of the church's ministers and members had been carried away by the dissimulation.[345] The schism ("cutting"), however, was not clean and continued to tear the body of the church in the following months. Malicious gossip and hateful misinformation continued to plague the church and brought to shame many of those who professed to be Christians.[346] Lawsuits followed over property disputes in several places, and ripped apart several more congregations.[347] Murray commented to the press that the schism was especially contradictory at a time when most Pentecostals were hearing a call to greater love and unity.[348]

"A Paradigm Shift"

Since 1923 the church had gradually developed a highly centralized system of government that made ministry depend too much on the plans and objectives of the general offices. Local churches were organized in great measure to raise funds for the support of the church's elaborate headquarters in Cleveland.[349] The new administration saw the mistake in this approach and began to shift the emphasis on ministry and evangelism to the local churches.[350]

Concurrent with this "paradigm shift," the infra-structure at headquarters began to be reorganized.[351] The venue of the Assembly was changed in 1992 from its familiar surroundings in Cleveland to Louisville, Kentucky, and scheduled to convene every two years instead of the traditional annual event.[352] The rapidity and magnitude of these changes became confusing to the ministers and churches, who had been accustomed to working within the old framework of the organization. Long-standing institutions and traditions have not been easy to give up, and thus the expected benefits from the new approach to fulfilling the church's global mission are still forthcoming, particularly in the United States and Canada.

New Financial System

Consistent with the new focus on local churches, the Ways and Means Committee presented to the 1992 Assembly a major plan of reform for the financial system.[353] The report in 1994 was even more radical, calling for changes that would directly effect the polity of the church. Accordingly, the former practice of distributing 20 percent of the local church's tithes to state and international offices was changed to 10 percent (to be achieved by a gradual reduction every two years until June 1, 1999).[354] Likewise, year-end surplus tithes was to be retained wholly in the local church by June 1, 1999.[355] Moreover, the practice of raising funds through the church's elaborate network of auxiliaries to swell the international treasury was reformed in order for discipling and ministry to be carried out primarily by the local churches. The Committee's report was rejected in 1994, pending further study. Finally, however, after further debate and clarification, the Assembly in 1996 accepted the new financial system.[356]

New System of Government

A significant move was made in 1990 when the new General Overseer appointed an International Committee to study the office of General Overseer. The study of this committee disagreed substantially with the traditional view of the office that developed between 1912-1915, and called for a reformation based on a plurality of leadership.[357] Murray himself did not understand the Committee's report, but he allowed the Questions and Subjects Committee to pursue the subject and to review the International Committee's report. The Questions and Subjects Committee concurred with the basic tenets of the International Committee's report, and in 1994 presented to the General Assembly a plan for reform.[358] The plan was accepted, and a special meeting of the presbytery was called in August 1997 to select a number of general presbyters to serve in the general oversight of the church.[359] In this historic meeting eight presbyters were selected, with more to be selected in the meeting scheduled for July 1998.[360] Among the plurality of presbyters who will share the office of General Overseer, three were selected to reside in Cleveland (not including Murray who retained his position). Others were selected to serve in Africa, Europe, the Middle East and Egypt, Asia and Oceana, Mexico, Central America and the Spanish-speaking Carribean, and South America.(The United States and Canada, and the English-speaking Carribean are pending further study and development.) The appointments are to take effect at the 1998 Assembly scheduled to convene in Fort Worth, Texas.

At The Moment

Opening the doors for progress in the church has not been without a heavy price to pay. Changes that were meant to be only modifications of traditional views have been taken by some to the extreme. Old standards of modesty have been blurred; and new liberties granted to the local churches have been abused by some acting independently. The church is still in transition and unsettled. Many of the new forms for government, education, and finance are still untried and pending success or failure; and thus many are anxious about sailing in uncharted waters.

The church is still working its way through an identity crisis, occasioned in part by refocusing traditional perceptions of the church's history relative to Tomlinson's experience on Burger Mountain, and in part by the magnitude of changes introduced by the new administration since 1990. Time will be needed for the revolutionary changes to be appreciated and effectively implemented or reformed. Yet, in spite of all that has transpired in recent years, the church has grown substantially, particularly in Asia, India, and Latin America. Murray's call in 1994 for the church to embrace "Turning to the Harvest" captured the imagination of the church and, for the moment, diverted attention away from its internal differences. But undercurrents of unrest and dissatisfaction soon surfaced again and continue to aggravate the peace and harmony of the church. Yet the church continues to seek to reconcile "all things" to Christ—desperately "[contending] for the faith once delivered to the saints." The final chapters of the Church of God of Prophecy remain to be written; but it is proceeding with an old conviction: that if it obeys its divine call, God has ordained its outcome in prophetic victory!

Notes

[1] Wade H. Phillips, **The Nature of the Church** (Cleveland, TN: WWPH, 1989), 37-54.

[2] Ibid, 45-48.

[3] With the exception of a few points regarding the exclusiveness of the Church of God of Prophecy and the tradition that developed from A. J. Tomlinson's Burger Mountain experience, which this present work attempts to correct [see p.26 and notes 216-221], Wade H. Phillips, **Mysterious Babylon and the Church of God** (Cleveland , TN: WWPH, 1982) is worth considering in regard to the church in prophecy and its historical development. See also Wade H. Phillips, **The Church in History and Prophecy** (Cleveland, TN: WWPH, 1990).

[4] It should be noted that many prophecies that have a primary fulfillment in Israel have two and sometimes three-fold meanings and applications which extend to the New Testament church. The great Wesleyan scholar and commentator, Adam Clarke, has argued convincingly on this point in regard to the nature of Hebrew literature and prophecy. See his comments, e.g., on the "Introduction to the Book of Isaiah," **Clarke's Commentary,** Vol.4, (Nashville: Abingdon Press), 7-16. Thus, the strict and static dispensational dichotomy between Israel and the church cannot be maintained when intrepreting the prophetical writings, for some prophecies have an extended application and fulfillment in the New Testament church.

[5] Phillips, **Mysterious Babylon,** 45-101; and see Melvin Hyatt and Rob Allen, **History of Christianity** (Cleveland, TN: WWPH, 1984), 76-80.

[6] Again Adam Clarke's comments are noteworthy on Isaiah 60. He maintains that the prophecy in this chapter is too glorious and majestic to have been fulfilled in the first century church; and rather sees the passage as a prophecy which predicted the church's fall and glorious restoration in the last days **Commentary,** Vol. 4, 222-224.

[7] For a comprehensive view of the Reformation from the perspective of the Anabaptist-Mennonite Movement, see **The Mennonite Encyclopedia**, 4 Vols. (Scottdale, PA: Mennonite Publishing Company), 1959; and for a more concise but excellent view of the origins and early development of the Anabaptists, see William R. Estep, **The Anabaptist Story,** (Nashville: Broadman Press, 1963).

[8]For an overview of Anabaptist ideas on the development of America and the Church of God, see Wade H. Phillips, "The Church of God: a Portrait of America," thesis presented to the Church of God School of Theology in partial fulfillment of Master's Degree, 1993.

[9]Recent research has shown clearly that Richard Spurling and Richard G. Spurling were not senior and junior in the formal sense of their names. The son's middle name was Green (hence Richard G. Spurling), whereas the father had no middle name (hence Richard Spurling). This has been established by studying more than fifty original documents—deeds, marriage certificates, census records, church minutes and records—which always carefully maintain the distinction. The father is never identified with a "G" after his first name, and the son is never without it; neither does the father ever use "Sr." after his name, nor the son "Jr." This distinction was also carefully maintained by Tomlinson in **The Last Great Conflict** (Cleveland, TN: The Press of Walter E. Rogers, 1913), 205-209. But for some reason historians later presumed that the two Spurlings were senior and junior in the formal sense of their names, and this presumption caused them to misinterpret Tomlinson's history, which had served as the basis for their own. E. L. Simmons, **History of the Church of God** (Cleveland, TN: COGPH, 1938); Charles W. Conn, **Like A Mighty Army** (Cleveland, TN: Pathway Press, 1955); and Charles T. Davidson, **Upon This Rock** (Cleveland,TN: WWPH, 1973), all make this mistake. And so with every writer thereafter. Once it is established that Richard G. Spurling is the son, not the father, Tomlinson's short history reads completely different than what historians had presumed. His account carefully maintains that the son was the primary architect and visionary of Christian Union. He was the one who prayed and studied so intensely beginning in 1884; and he preached the revolutionary sermon on August 19, 1886, to which his father, wife, and six others responded by covenanting together to form Christian Union. And it was the son who served as the church's first pastor. These facts are further substantiated by the carefully maintained distinction between Richard G. Spurling's status as a licensed minister in contrast to the ordained status of his father, Richard Spurling. Thus, "Elder Richard Spurling was duly acknowledged and

recognized as their minister [not pastor], to do all the business devolved on him as such in the new order. He then . . . took his seat as moderator, and by prayer dedicated the infant church of God . . . An invitation was then given for the reception of members, and they received Richard G. Spurling, who was then a licensed minister. The church chose him as their pastor, and had him ordained the next month, September 26, 1886" [**Conflict,** 207].

[10]A. J. Tomlinson, **The Last Great Conflict,** 205; Richard G. Spurling, **The Lost Link** (Turtletown, TN: 1920), 1-7, 35-37.

[11]For an understanding of Landmarkism, see G. H. Orchard, **A Concise History of the Foreign Baptists** (Nashville: Graves & Marks, Ag'ts of Tenn. Publication Society, 1855); and notice particularly J. R. Graves' "Introductory Essay," i-xxiii. See also J. R. Graves, **Old Landmarkism: What Is It?**, (Texarkana, TX: Bogard Press, 1880 reprint); and John T. Christian, **A History of the Baptists** (Texarkana, TX: Bogard Press, 1922). For the way that Landmarkism affected the Spurlings, see Wade H. Phillips, "Richard Spurling and the Baptist Roots of the Church of God," paper presented to the Twenty-Third Annual Conference of the Society for Pentecostal Studies, Guadalahara, Mexico, November 11-13, 1993, 16-26.

[12]**Lost Link**, 32; and Phillips, "Baptist Roots," 22-31.

[13]Ibid, 25-28; **Conflict,** 205-208.

[14]Ibid, 16, 23-25.

[15]Ibid, 23-26.

[16]Ibid, 2-6, 16, 20-21, 27-28.

[17]**Conflict,** 206-208.

[18]Ibid, 207.

[19]Ibid.

[20]Ibid, 208; and see note 9.

[21]Ibid.

[22]*Holly Springs Baptist Church Minutes,* September-November, 1886; and see Phillips, "Baptist Roots," 34-37.

[23]Census Record, Monroe County, TN, 1880; Nancy Jane (Norman) Spurling, Richard's wife, died in June, 1878. She is buried in the Dehart cemetery in Monroe County, less than a mile from the Holly Springs Church. Richard died on March 26, 1891 in Anderson County, TN (*Clinton Gazette,* April 2, 1891). See Phillips, "Baptist Roots," 36-37.

[24]Most records show Richard G. Spurling's birth was on July 28, 1858, including his tombstone at Turtletown, TN; but

July 28, 1857 is the correct date. This has been confirmed recently in a letter written to Tomlinson by Spurling's own hand, dated November 6, 1932. He says, "Well as for my age I was 75 this past July 28." This is also the date given by his son, Pinkney, in his *Biographical Sketch of the Reverend R. G. Spurling,* 1 (WHPC).

[25]This has been determined by elucidating the data from several sources, including interviews [1982-1995] with Richard G. Spurling's granddaughter, Allie (Spurling) Ledford (1913-). She lived with her grandparents for nineteen years, and resides today at the old Spurling homeplace in Turtletown, TN. Besides her long and intimate relationship with her grandparents, Mrs. Ledford is a pious Christian and thus an excellent witness. Her testimony has confirmed the scenario given in Pinkney Spurling's biographical sketch of his father's life and ministry. Pinkney's data and Mrs. Ledford's testimony correspond also with deed records that show when and where Richard G. Spurling lived between 1857 and 1902. Pinkney was born in 1877 and was thus an "eyewitness" to the developments in his father's ministry. His work is poorly written, but has become a valuable source in constructing the history of events between 1886 and 1902. Evidently, the Barney Creek Church dispersed as early as 1889. Deed records show that Richard Spurling sold the property at Barney Creek in February 1889. Pinkney's record shows that about this same time his father "went over near the center of Monroe County, Tennessee, to a place called Piney and set a church in order" (*Sketch*,9) A little later he notes, "Years later they choose [sic] to be independent" (Ibid). This data corresponds with Joe Abbott's **The Forgotten Church,** (Bridgeport, AL, 1962), n.p (WHPC, xerox copy), written from information given primarily by R. G. Spurling's son, Richard Eli [b.1884]. This work fills in several names which are correspondent with other records in the church's history, and with federal census records and county marriage records. Amazingly, this church is still in existence today in approximately the same place it was in 1890. It is located at Pine Ridge on the old Reliance Road about eight miles southwest of Barney Creek. Charlie Freeman [1902-] and Joshua Prock [1905-] were active in this church when they were children (interviews by Wade H. Phillips, 1992-1995).

Charlie (who pastored the church himself for several years) is well rehearsed with the church's beginnings and confirmed that R. G. Spurling had organized it. Charlie's uncle, Andrew Freeman, was apparently the first pastor (1890-1910); and his father, James Wesley Freeman (1879-1949) pastored it after Andrew died. Andrew and James were ordained by Spurling. Dorcas Freeman, Andrew's and James' sister, was licensed also by Spurling to preach (according to Freeman, interview 1994). This corresponds with Richard G. Spurling's letter to A. J. Tomlinson (dated, November 6, 1932), which shows that he had ordained five or six ministers before Tomlinson in 1903 ["I think you were the fifth or sixth preacher I ordained," WHPC], and also with the fact that Andrew Freeman is recognized as an elder in the first Assembly in 1906 (*General Assembly Minutes, 1906-1914*), Photographic Reproductions of the First Ten General Assemblies (Cleveland, TN: WWPH, 1992), 15, 18-19. The others may have been Andy Paul and Joe Tipton according to Freeman. (His testimony corresponds with **The Forgotten Church**, 14-15. Andy Paul married Andrew's and James' sister, Sarah; thus the church was largely an entended family congregation, which corresponds with Pinkney's testimony). We know, of course, that Spurling ordained W. F. Bryant, Jr. as a deacon on May 15, 1902 and probably William M. Coleman on June 13, 1903, the same day that Tomlinson joined the church and was ordained. Andrew Freeman [1871-1910] is buried near Nancy J. Spurling (Richard G. Spurling's mother) in the Dehart cemetery, and was married to the sister of Richard Spurling's grandson's wife (*Spurling Genealogical Record*, WHPC). Several of the members of this church lived on Steer Creek which was later visited and evangelized by M. S. Lemons 1908-1909 (*General Assembly Minutes 1906- 1914*, 57). Evidently the church had decided to go independent according to Pinkney's *Sketch* (above), which seems also to be implicit in Lemons' report (*General Assembly Minutes 1906-1914*, 57). This was also confirmed by Freeman and Prock (Phillips interview, 1994). Joseph ("Joe") Tipton was active in this church also according to Freeman and Prock (Ibid).

After Spurling organized the second Christian Union congregation at Pine Ridge, he apparently organized one on

"Paul's Mountain" (local designation in reference to Andy Paul's family) about three miles from the Pine Ridge church (**The Forgotten Church**, 27-29). Several of the members of this church lived between Paul's Mountain near Spurling's old home place and Barney Creek (interviews Freeman and Prock, 1992-1994). The descendants of Charlie and Joshua still live in the vicinity. Both of these churches were called "Christian Union" until 1907 when they adopted the name, Church of God. This was occasioned by the preaching of Joe Tipton (Freeman interview, 1994), which corresponds with the year that the church officially adopted the name, Church of God, in the General Assembly. Not surprisingly Tipton was scheduled to be on the program at the second Assembly in 1907 (Program Schedule, WHPC). Both churches rejected the idea and government of the General Assembly, and thereafter called the churches that made up the Assembly the "Assembly churches" (Freeman interview, 1994), which explains why they are not mentioned by the time that Tomlinson writes his history in 1912. (But it also explains why Lemons is working in the area in 1909. Freeman remembers attending a meeting on Steer Creek about 1909-1910 with Spurling, Tomlinson, Bryant, and his uncle Andrew present [interview,1994]). Tomlinson quite apparently reconstructed the early history of the church according to his experience and purpose after he joined it in 1903, and particularly in light of the nature and purpose of the church as it was transformed by the institution of the General Assembly.

During the time that Spurling had organized these churches he had evidently moved his family to Polk County near the Cherokee County line on the north side of the Hiwassee River. Deed records in Polk County show that Richard purchased this land from his father-in-law, Killis Hamby, in 1890. This move was occasioned, evidently, by his father selling the property on Barney Creek in February 1889. Thereafter, Richard built a house and gristmill and, apparently either before or shortly after he moved, organized a church near his home with "five or six members" (Bryant and Lemons interview, Document 27-A, p.3). Mrs. Ledford (see above) remembers this as the old homeplace. Her grandparents moved back into the old homeplace for awhile when she was a child [1918-1921], while Spurling helped to build a log flume for a lumber company operation in the area. (Mrs.Ledford traveled with the writer in November 1993 and showed him the location of "the old homeplace" and where she thought the gristmill had been located). This perfectly corresponds with Pinkney's account: "In 1889 we moved to Polk County where Father had organized a church sometime before. While we lived there this church did good and prospered . . . But school facilities were bad there for us children, so Father . . . went to Turtletown in Polk County and bought a farm where schools were convenient. He still kept watch over the work even though it was small, taking nothing from them for services, but he helped them" (*Sketch*, 9). According to deed records Spurling bought the Turtletown farm in 1893. Evidently he continued to pastor this church after he moved, and this church was part of the covenant community Spurling mentions in 1895 **(Lost Link,** 45). Moreover, this is apparently the church that Bryant attempted to help Spurling revive, which later "went dead." (Bryant and Lemons interview, Document 27-A, p.3).

[26]Ibid.

[27]**Conflict,** 207; **Lost Link,** 22-23, 42, 45, and compare G. H. Orchard's history. See Phillips, "Baptist Roots," 18-19n51.

[28]See note 25.

[29]Though these churches remained independent, nevertheless, several of the members continued to attend the General Assemblies through the years, and even performed musical programs on occasion (Freeman interview, 1994, and reports in *Chattanooga Free Press*, September 1938).

[30]*The Way of Faith* (Columbia, S.C.) often published Irwin's itinerary between 1895-1898, which shows his activity in the South. Irwin's own periodical, *Lives Coals of Fire* (Lincoln, NE), shows clearly the development of the movement from 1898-1900; see also Harold D. Hunter, "Beniah, TN: A Case of the Vanishing Flame," unpublished manuscript, 1994 (Xerox copy, WHPC).

[31]This is now clear from all reports. The revival first broke out in Monroe County where William B. Martin, Joseph M. Tipton, Milton McNabb, Billy Hamby, and Frank Porter lived. Spurling's congregations, not bound by the restrictions of a creed, freely accepted the new doctrine and were

swept into the movement. Charlie Freeman testified that the movement began in 1895 and Christian Union congregations became the hotbed from which the movement flourished in Tennessee and North Carolina (interview, May 1992). This testimony corresponds with earlier accounts of the movement, including "History of Pentecost," *The Faithful Standard,* September, 1922, 5-6, 20-21 (WHPC). See also Hunter, "Beniah," 22-29.

[32]**Conflict**, 209-210; "History of Pentecost" *Faithful Standard* (September 1922), 6, 20.

[33]Tomlinson only mentions Martin, McNabb, and Tipton **(Conflict**, 209-210). Bryant adds Billy Hamby (Bryant and Lemons, document 27-A, p.2), and Lemons implicates R. Frank Porter (Ibid.). Hamby was Spurling's brother-in-law. He is buried in the Dehart cemetery in Monroe County near Holly Springs Baptist Church. Tipton and McNabb were members of the Rural Vale Baptist Church just across the hill from Holly Springs on the old Reliance Road (Charlie Freeman interview, 1994). The fact that Tipton is buried in the Rural Vale cemetery seems to confirm Freeman's testimony. The Rural Vale church is still active, located only about two miles from Richard Spurling's 1860 homeplace (1860 Monroe County tax records and federal census records). Billy Martin is buried in the old Methodist cemetery at Ironsburg, and Milton McNabb is buried in California (McNabb Genealogical Records, WHPC).

[34]**Conflict**, 210; "History of Pentecost," *Faithful Standard* (September, 1922), 5-6, 20-21.

[35]In recent years we have obtained xerox copies of the original minutes and records of the Liberty and Pleasant Hill Baptist Churches (WHPC). These have provided valuable data to confirm and clarify for the first time oral reports of Church of God history. See also Phillips, "Baptist Roots," 37-39.

[36]**Conflict,** 210-213.

[37]Ibid, 211-212; "History of Pentecost" *Faithful Standard* (September 1922), 20-21. Charles W. Conn, **Like A Mighty Army,** 29- 37; Wade H. Phillips, "Our Rich Church of God Heritage: Born of the Spirit," *Church of God History & Heritage* (Cleveland, TN: Pathway Press, Summer, 1997) 1; Pinkney Spurling, *Sketch,* 9.

[38]**Conflict,** 210-211; *Sketch,* 8; "History of Pentecost," *Faithful Standard* (September, 1922), 20.

[39]Ibid, 212; "History of Pentecost," *Faithful Standard* (September 1922), 6; Hunter, "Beniah," 22-31.

[40]*Liberty Baptist Church Minutes*, December 1899-March 1901; *Pleasant Hill Baptist Church Minutes*, March 1899-May 1901; *Liberty & Ducktown Baptist Association Minutes*, October 1898 under "Resolution One"; Nettie Bryant interview, document 8-A, pp. 3-4 (WHPC).

[41]**Conflict,** 212; **Like A Mighty Army**, 44-45; W. F. Bryant, Jr., letter to Sister Bowling, dated October 8, 1947, says "there were about 18-20" [WHPC].

[42]In his annual address in 1928, Tomlinson reflected, " . . . in nineteen years the Church of God was built up from one church with a membership of sixteen, to . . . a membership of 21,076" **Historical Annual Addresses,** Vol.2 (Cleveland,TN: WWPH, 1971 p.13). The sixteen members refers to the charter members of the Holiness Church at Camp Creek in 1902. Bryant remembered "about seventeen members," "A Little Church History," *The Lighted Pathway*, November 8, 1941, p. 7. Tomlinson's account is preferred, for he knew the importance of maintaining precise historical accounts, particularly dates and figures, and because he is definite on the number.

[43]**Lost Link,** 22-23, 42; and see note 25.

[44]The principle adopted in the first Assembly—"We do not consider ourselves a legislative or executive body, but judicial only"—was often repeated and carefully maintained for many years. Further, the need for the local churches to ratify Assembly resolutions was taken seriously for many years. The Assembly was clearly understood to be a voluntary association of individual churches, particularly by Spurling; though Tomlinson may have envisioned the Assembly as a centralized and authoritarian council. Yet even in 1916 he acknowledged, "We have been following too closely, I fear, after the idea of each church being an independent government of its own and bordering on to [*sic*] independent democracy instead of real Bible theocracy" [**Historical Annual Addresses,** Vol.1, 70-71].

[45]A. J. Tomlinson, **Answering the Call of God** (Cleveland, TN: WWPH), 4-6. Tomlinson does not give the exact year of his conversion but says sometime during "the first year of my married life" (Ibid,4) [I] began to pray [he was married on April 24, 1889]. This was without results at first but he "never let up until [he] got a real experience of salvation"

(Ibid,5). His experience of sanctification happened "some little time later" (Ibid). This seems to correspond to his son Homer's account for his conversion in July 1892 **Diary of A. J. Tomlinson,** Vol. 1 (New York, published by the editor, 1949, 10). Tomlinson's reference to his sanctification experience "about twenty years ago" (**Conflict,** 226) would date his experience in 1892, since he wrote this work in 1912. His reflection in his 1925 annual address to "thirty-two years of service" [which puts the date at 1893], and "thirty years" without secular employment except for about three months late in 1902 at Elwood, Indiana (**Diary,** May 10, 1903), is probably a reference to his call into the ministry, rather than the year of his conversion (**Historical Annual Addresses**, Vol.1, 259).

[46]**Answering the Call,** 5.

[47]A. J. Tomlinson, **Diary,** May-October 1899. But he evidently had visited the mountains at least twice before moving to Culberson in October 1899. Homer A. Tomlinson, ed., **Diary of A. J. Tomlinson**, Vol.1, 17.

[48]**Answering the Call,** 16-18; "R. G. Spurling Passes Over the Tide," *White Wing Messenger*, June 10, 1935, 1,4.

[49]**Conflict,** 158-159; **Diary**, June 13, 1903; **Answering the Call,** 18; and see notes 216-217.

[50]"R. G. Spurling Passes Over the Tide," *White Wing Messenger*, June 10, 1935, 4; **Answering the Call,** 18; and see notes 216-221.

[51] **Conflict**, 214.

[52]Ibid. This made a total of thirty-five. The church was organized with sixteen charter members, five were added on June 13, 1903, and fourteen more added during the course of the year.

[53]He moved to Cleveland in December 1904 (**Diary,** November- December 1904) but continued to pastor the Camp Creek church and attended the work he had begun at Culberson.

[54]**Conflict**, 210-212; estimates of how many were baptized in the Spirit exceeded one hundred persons (Ibid,212); but see Hunter, "Beniah," 22-31. A close scrutiny of all the records indicates that this number was probably inflated. The distinction of speaking in tongues as a necessary evidence of Spirit-baptism was apparently not closely adhered to in the estimates. Evidently many who were blessed or moved by the Spirit in some manner [shouting,

screaming, dancing, leaping, falling prostrate] though they had not spoken in tongues were counted among the number of them whom were Spirit-baptized. W. F. Bryant's wife and two of his daughters, who were present and active in the revival during and after 1896, admitted that they had not heard tongues-speech until after they arrived in Cleveland in 1907 (interview, Document 8-A; and Nora Bryant Jones interview by Harold D. Hunter 10-5-1992, "Beniah," 14n 38). Bryant himself was ambiguous in his comments and recollections about dates, and the sequence of events and their significance.

[55]"History of Pentecost," *Faithful Standard* (September 1922, 5- 6) submits to the Azusa Street meeting in Los Angeles as the beginning of the modern Pentecostal movement. Tomlinson, even in 1912, credits W. J. Seymour, the pastor of the Azusa Street mission, with the restoration of the doctrine of speaking in tongues as the evidence of Spirit-baptism [**Conflict**, 156-157].

[56]**Conflict,** 233; *The Bridegroom's Messenger*, 1:6, January 15, 1908, p.2.

[57]Ibid, 233-236.

[58]Tomlinson, Diary, August 9-October 14 1908; and see Homer A. Tomlinson, ed., **Diary of A. J. Tomlinson**, Vol.1, 24-32; and **Like A Mighty Army,** 86-92.

[59]*The Journal and Banner*, September 17, 1908, p.3.

[60]The best source for an overview of the rapid spread of Pentecostalism throughout the Southeast is *The Bridegroom's Messenger*. This was a bi-monthly publication that G. B. Cashwell began from Atlanta in October 1907. It is a virtual journal of the Pentecostal movement in the South between 1907-1910 (Xerox copies, WHPC).

[61]Cp. 1907 and 1911 General Assembly Minutes *[General Assembly Minutes 1906-1914]*.

[62]J. H. Simpson (1865-1936) had met Tomlinson shortly after he had moved from McMinn County to Cleveland in 1905 (letter from Simpson to Tomlinson, March 1, 1909, WHPC). He had been connected with the fire-baptized holiness movement at least by 1902. Two of his daughters had married the sons of Milton McNabb, all of whom were active in the movement (Genealogical Records of Elias Milton McNabb and Jacob H.Simpson, WHPC). Simpson's eldest daughter, Minnie, had written an article in *The Way* (March 1905). Soon after Simpson moved to Cleveland he

established a general mercantile located at 101 East Central Avenue, dealing in "dry goods, shoes, and groceries" (specified on the letterhead of his business stationary, WHPC). The name of his business was "J. H. Simpson & Son." He began to worship with Tomlinson in private homes, and became a charter member of the Holiness Church in Cleveland when it was organized on October 10, 1906. He was ordained shortly thereafter as a deacon and became extremely active and prominent in the church with his wife, Julia, and fifteen children. He paid the token fee of one dollar [a legal formality] for the land donated to the church on the corner of Eleventh and Peoples Streets (Testimony of Ethel [Simpson] Robertson, November 18, 1984, WHPC), and contributed substantially in time and labor as well as finances to the construction of their house of worship in 1907 (Tomlinson, **Diary**, February 1, 1909; Letter from Simpson to Tomlinson, March 1, 1909, WHPC). Nevertheless, Tomlinson received complaints constantly against Simpson's apparent harshness and domineering spirit. Simpson's relationship with the church's prominent leaders—W. F. Bryant, M. S. Lemons, H. L. Trim—became strained and difficult (Letter from Eva M. [Simpson] Crittenden to Tomlinson, March 2, 1909, WHPC). This all became more magnified after Pentecost came to Cleveland in 1908. Simpson never got in the spirit of it, rejected the revival from the beginning and grew sour. Tomlinson noted, "J. H. Simpson has been causing us trouble by division and offences and contentions for several months" (**Diary,** January 2, 1909). His tendency to be legalistic and harsh showed up all the more against the joy and glory of the Pentecostal manifestations that filled the church. The church had grown from sixty members late in 1907 to more than two hundred by October 1908, and Simpson and his family were left behind clinging to a pre-Pentecostal mind-set. Unwilling to submit to the new light, he rose against it with a vengeance and created great havoc in the church (Ibid). Finally, on January 2, 1909, only four days before the fourth General Assembly, Simpson was brought before the church in conference (Ibid). After "considerable persuasion" by Tomlinson, with tears and agonizing prayer by the church to no avail, he was excluded based on the instruction in Romans 16:17 (Ibid). Simpson did not accept the decision lightly, and began to campaign against the church. He and his family sent a barrage of harsh letters to Tomlinson, accusing Tomlinson himself of being unjust and a lord, and charging Bryant and others with various indiscretions, including abuse of their trust as stewards. Further he threatened to sue the church if he was not reinstated (Letters by J. H. Simpson to Tomlinson, January 30, Feburary 2, 22, March 1, 1909; Mammie and Ethel Simpson to Tomlinson January 31, 1909; Julia Simpson to Tomlinson, n.d.; Eva M. [Simpson] Crittenden to Tomlinson, March 2, 1909; WHPC).

John B. Goins had been baptized in the Spirit on July 18, 1906 in Griffin, Georgia. Shortly thereafter his minister's license was revoked and he was excluded from his denomination (*The Bridegroom's Messenger*, 1:2, p.2). He then began an independent Pentecostal church at Florence, Alabama in 1907 (Ibid). He came in contact with Church of God ministers about that time, and while attending a Pentecostal convention in Memphis was ordained by Tomlinson and L. P. Adams on November 22, 1908 (Tomlinson, **Diary,** November 26, 1908; John B. Goins' *Certificate of Ordination*, WHPC). On April 15 of the next year Tomlinson conducted a revival at Goins' church in Florence (Ibid, April 15, 1909) and, apparently, made arrangements at that time to bring Goins to Cleveland to assist in the work there. Goins was fairly well-educated and extremely zealous for the new Pentecostal experience and message, and thus seemed to be a promising minister for the church. However, when he arrived in Cleveland in August 1909 (*Cleveland Herald*, January 13, 1909) he was met with the trouble still brewing over Simpson's exclusion from the church. Doubtlessly Simpson's influence magnified what already seemed to Goins to be fanatical behavior among the leaders and members in the Cleveland church [including Tomlinson, Bryant, and Lemons](Ibid). Further, he disagreed with the doctrine that the church is a visible body formalized by a church covenant (Letter from Goins to Tomlinson April 1910, WHPC). Before he came to Cleveland he had written in *The Bridegroom's Messenger* "There is not a council of men on earth today that is able to set down rules to write out a discipline that will be able to govern the church of God. Men have tried to do that but have failed"

(2:30, January 15, 1909,2). Eventually Goins recanted his Pentecostal testimony, denounced speaking in tongues at any time without an interpreter, questioned the operation of spiritual gifts in general, and denied that tongues-speech was a necessary evidence of Spirit-baptism (Ibid; Letters from Simpson to Tomlinson, January 30, March 2, 1909; Duggar, *A. J. Tomlinson*, 84; and see Homer A. Tomlinson, *The Great Vision of the Church of God*, published by the author, 1939, 10). During the course of these things in Cleveland, serious accusations [of adultery] against Goins were coming to Tomlinson's office from the church he left at Florence (Noah Patrick, Oak Waldrep, Joe Patrick to Tomlinson, August 11, 1909; Noah Patrick to Tomlinson, August 15, 1909; P. E. Cramblit to Tomlinson, August 23 and September 3, 1909; L. O. Waldrep to Tomlinson, December 13, 1909, WHPC). These accusations were supported by messages and interpretations, which Tomlinson questioned (Letter from Tomlinson to Noah Patrick, Oak Waldrep, and Joe Patrick, August 30, 1909, WHPC). To what extent these things pushed Goins further in the direction that he already was headed—to recant his Pentecostal experience and rebel against the government of the church—we cannot be sure; but certainly it bore heavily upon him (Letter from Goins to P. E. Cramblit, August 16, 1909). In any case, Goins gravitated toward Simpson and his faction and soon realized complete affinity with them and became their leader. This was an opening for which Simpson had eagerly awaited. While Tomlinson was in Florida Goins denounced him as a heretic, went through the motions of revoking his ministry, and had him "expelled" from the church (Homer, **Diary**, Vol.1, 85-89; **The Great Vision**, 10). Now working closely with Simpson, P. A. Wingo, Ralph Aikman, and others, Goins was making every effort to seize control of the church (Tomlinson, **Diary,** November 10, 1909). A. J. Lawson, Bryant, Lemons, Mary Jane and Homer, all wrote to Tomlinson about the trouble advising him to return home as soon as possible (Homer, **Diary,** Vol.1, 74-80) [Note: Bryant was illiterate and thus dictated his letter via Homer]. During the confrontational business conference that followed about forty-three stood with Goins, whereupon Goins turned in his license to Tomlinson and declared independence (Tomlinson, **Diary,** December 1, 1909). Tomlinson went home and burned Goins' license (Ibid). A terrible struggle followed [turned into a physical brawl at one point] that wound up in the courts and brought to shame the name of the church ("Holiness Preachers In Toils Of The Law," *The Journal and Banner*, July 23, 1909; "Holiness Preachers Appeal Case To Court," Ibid, July 27, 1909). The court ruled that the Goins-Simpson faction could use the church's facilities every other week. This was unacceptable to Tomlinson and the church, but the situation continued for nearly a year before the church finally won the legal right to have complete control of the building again (Lillie Duggar, **A. J. Tomlinson,** Cleveland,TN: WWPH, 1964, 82-86; and Homer, **Diary,** Vol. 1, 88-89). Goins returned to Florence, Alabama, and proceeded to divide the church there at Sunnyside. He named his independent organization, Sunnyside Street Holiness Church (Letter from Goins to Tomlinson, March 30, 1910). Goins came back to Tomlinson thirty years later, made restitution to the church, and re-joined on March 26, 1939 (Tomlinson, **Diary,** March 30, 1939). However, within a few days he regressed to his old complaints about fanaticism and on April 10th was again excluded from the church (Ibid, April 5,14, 1939; and see Homer, **Diary,** Vol.1, 89). Simpson remained in Cleveland, became active in politics and died on November 3, 1936. He is buried in Fort Hill cemetery near Tomlinson (Jacob H. Simpson File, WHPC).

[63]Letter from J. H. Simpson to Tomlinson, February 2, 1909. "Brother Sperling sed [*sic*] you had no rite [*sic*]to turn me out and I can prove that by him and others."

[64]See note 62.

[65]*General Assembly Minutes 1906-1914*, 85-87.

[66]Ibid, 85-91

[67]**Conflict,** 214-215.

[68]The endorsement reads, "We the undersigned in conference held at Union Grove, Tenn. Jan. 12, 1907 endorse the credentials of the above date and signature and hereby set our hands and subscribe to the same." It was signed by Elders W. F. Bryant, M. S. Lemons, A. J. Tomlinson, Clerk (Xerox copy, WHPC).

[69]Letter from Lee to Mrs. W. D. Clark, Galloway, FL., July 13, 1926: "The Church of God, in its present existence was set in order January 26, 1906, in the home of J. C. Murphy, Cherokee County, North Carolina."

[70]This was certainly the position of Richard G. Spurling, J. L. Scott, Sam C. Perry, and others.

[71]Wade H. Phillips, "Quakerism and Frank W. Sandford: Major Influences that Transformed A. J. Tomlinson and the Church of God," paper presented to the Twenty-First Annual Conference of the Society For Pentecostal Studies, Lakeland, FL., 1991, 2-7.

[72]He was educated at Westfield Indiana's renowned Union Academy (Homer, **Diary** ,Vol.1, 11). This school was rated as one of the best high schools in America in the late nineteenth century. John J. Baldwin wrote early in the century, "One can hardly find a locality between the Atlantic and the Pacific where there is not someone who has heard of Westfield and Union high" (John F. Haines, **History of Hamilton County**, Indiana, 1915, 31). Haines noted that "many graduates of Union High were as proud of their credentials as if they had graduated from Harvard, Yale, or Princeton. Records do show that men and women of 'great moral fiber' did go out from the school to fill with distinction positions of honor and responsibility in life" (Ibid, 33). See also **Answering the Call of God,** 3; "Union High School Graduation Program," 1883, WHPC; Letter by Byford F. Inman, Westfield, IN, July, 23, 1927, WHPC; "The Aurora," 1:1, Union High School paper, 1899, WHPC.

[73]**Conflict,** 91, 127-129, 236-240.

[74]Ibid.

[75]See *General Assembly Minutes 1906-1914*, 257-263, 296-309; and Phillips, "Quakerism and Frank W. Sandford: Major Influences that Tranformed A. J. Tomlinson and the Church of God"; and **The Corruption of the Noble Vine,** 10-35.

[76]*General Assembly Minutes 1906-1914*, 265, 313-314.

[77]Ibid, 314-315.

[78]In his nineteenth annual address in 1929 Tomlinson rehearsed how the office of General Overseer had developed, showing that he had been selected by the Assembly year after year by unanimous agreement. But in 1913, he notes, "When the time came for the selection of the General Overseer that year, the Holy Ghost seemed to wrest it out of the hands of the Assembly and took such complete charge of the affairs until it was believed, by perhaps all present, that the Overseer had been selected by the Holy Ghost and anointed for the position. Then the next year the Holy Spirit . . . made it so clear that the selection was final that

I was afraid to mention it any more for fear I would grieve the Holy Ghost" (**Historical Annual Addresses**, Vol. 2, 53).

[79]*General Assembly Minutes 1906-1914*, 107-109.

[80]Ibid, 267, 270.

[81]Churches that were mature and strong enough continued to call their own pastors, but in many cases the state overseers began to appoint pastors after the Ninth Assembly in 1913. Note the decision by Tomlinson (Ibid, 270).

[82]**Lost Link,** 52.

[83]Phillips, "Quakerism and Frank W. Sandford: Major Influences that Transformed A. J. Tomlinson and the Church of God," 1-10; **The Corruption of the Noble Vine,** 1-180; Homer, **Diary,** Vo.1, 7-8, 16.

[84]See note 72.

[85]Homer, **Diary,** Vol.1, 7-17; Phillips, **Corruption,** 1-180; "Transformed Tomlinson," 1-10.

[86]Besides the record we have in Tomlinson's **Diary** and his short history in **The Last Great Conflict**, we have discovered recently a report written in Tomlinson's own hand (August 16, 1904) that fills in much of the activity of the church between 1903-1904. This report evidently was never published (Xerox copy, WHPC).

[87]The best source to see this development is *The Bridegroom's Messenger*, all issues 1907-1910.

[88]Ibid; Tomlinson, **Diary,** 1907-1909; Homer, **Diary,** 7-8; Conn, **Like A Mighty Army**, 85-116.

[89]Stanley H. Frodsham, **With Signs Following**, re.ed. (Springfield, MO: Gospel Publishing House, 1946), 41-42. Much of Britton's ministry is chronicled thereafter in *The Bridegroom's Messenger*, 1907-1910.

[90]Tomlinson's "Address of Acceptance," *General Assembly Minutes 1906-1914*, 199: "In making the selection of the man to conduct one of the great campmeetings at Durant Fla. they wrote me that the Holy Ghost had named me as that man." Since Sam C. Perry was the president of the Pleasant Grove Campmeeting and Mrs. R. M. Evans was the secretary and treasurer, one of them probably wrote Tomlinson. And see notes 95-96.

[91]Tomlinson, **Diary,** October 9-November 26, 1909; Mr. and Mrs. Howard Juilerat, "Wonderful Meetings at Tampa and Pleasant Grove Camp Grounds, Florida" *The Bridegroom's Messenger*, 2:40, June 15, 1909, 1; though Tomlinson conflicted with F. M. Britton over the nature of the church

and the Spirit's operations. Britton at first denied that the church was visible and empowered with disciplinary authority. Dr. Conn notes that a pet slogan of Britton was "No card to sign, no church to 'jine', just come out from among them and be ye separate" (**Like A Mighty Army,** 97n12). Britton also at first resisted the gift of "interpretation of tongues." Homer gives a full report of Britton's differences with his father (**Diary**, Vol 1, 83- 85).

[92]See notes 90-91, and references on F. M. Britton and his influence above.

[93]Tomlinson, **Diary,** October-November, 1909; and **Like A Mighty Army,** 96-99.

[94]R. M. Evans, "Missionary," *The Evening Light and Church of God Evangel*, March 1, 1910, 7.

[95]*General Assembly Minutes 1906-1914*, 106-107, 129-130. Much of Evans' personal information comes from research done by James E. Cossey, which he compiled in a report in 1979, "Search for R. M. Evans" (Xerox copy, WHPC); see notes 96-97.

[96]*The Bridegroom's Messenger*, 1:13, 3. He had turned in his credentials to the Methodist Church and began to supervise a "little orphanage" at Pleasant Grove Campground (Ibid, and Cossey, "Search for R. M. Evans"). His wife served as secretary and treasurer for the Pleasant Grove Campmeeting in 1908-1909 and Sam C. Perry served as President (*The Bridegroom's Messenger* 2:34, March 15, 1909, 2). Evans evidently joined the Church of God when Tomlinson conducted the Campmeeting there in 1909. Tomlinson officially appointed Evans as missionary to the Bahamas sometime in 1910, and again in 1911 and 1912. Evans and some others were excluded from the church thereafter on some charge unknown to the writer at this time. They appealed to the Assembly through J. S. Llewellyn for their case to be reconsidered. After some discussion the Assembly authorized the General Overseer to investigate the matter [*General Assembly Minutes 1906-1914*, 321]. No data is available (known to the writer) that reveals the outcome.

[97]Tomlinson, **Diary,** January-April, 1911. Evans' report to the General Assembly in 1912 gives additional information (*General Assembly Minutes 1906-1914*, 129-130); and some further details about the missionary adventure are provided in Tomlinson's "Brief Sketch of the Life and

Works" of Roy C. Miller, **Classified Scriptures on the Church of God** (Cleveland,TN: Press of Church of God Evangel, 1913), 12-21.

[98]*General Assemnly Minutes 1906-1914*, 106-107.

[99]*Minutes of the Eighteenth Annual Assembly of the Church of God* (Cleveland, TN: CGPH, November 1-7, 1923), 47.

[100]Vinson Synan, **The Holiness-Pentecostal Movement in the United States** (Grand Rapids: Wm. B. Eerdmans, 1971), 80.

[101]Though only five feet seven inches in height and about 165 pounds, there seems to have been an aura about him that was striking. This was due in part to his personal charisma and integrity, but probably more so to his complete dedication to the ministry and his vision to build the Church of God. Consider, for example, the testimonies of so many of the church's early leaders (*General Assembly Minutes 1906-1914*, 265, 314-315). The real or imagined signs of divine approval upon his life and ministry were probably most impressive (Ibid; see also **Conflict,** 236-241).

[102]Perry had been appointed as overseer of Kentucky in 1911, and shortly thereafter located at London north Jellico. Llewellyn lived near Knoxville and attended the convention with Tomlinson. But J. B. Mitchell is probably the one who made contact with the Mountain Assembly body since he was staying at Jellico at that time (Tomlinson, **Diary,** October 9, 1911).

[103]*Minutes of the Fifth Annual Mountain Assembly of the Churches of God*, 2-5 (Xerox copy, WHPC). This Assembly was held at Siler Chapel, Polleyton, Kentucky, October 6-8, 1911. Tomlinson actually moderated the Assembly during the election of their Moderator (Ibid,2). For Tomlinson's viewpoint, see **Diary,** October 9, 1911, and *Church of God Evangel*, October 15, 1911. See also Luther Gibson, **History of the Church of God Mountain Assembly,**1954; 8-9 (WHPC); and Michael Padgett, **A Goodly Heritage** (Kearney, NE: Morris Publishing, 1995), 20-24.

[104]*General Assembly Minutes 1906-1914*, 140-141.

[105]The best explanation of this to date is Padgett, **A Goodly Heritage,** 20-24.

[106]Flora E. Bowers and Zetta A. Gamble, "Work in the Mountains of Tennessee," *The Bridegroom's Messenger*, 2:44, August 15, 1909, 2. Other issues show that funds were received.

[107]After the Campmeeting at Pleasant Grove in 1909 Tomlinson increasingly became distanced from G. B. Cashwell, F. M. Britton, J. H. King, and other Pentecostal pioneers. *The Bridegroom's Messenger* published a doctrinal definition of the Pentecostal Movement in May 1909 that included ten articles (2:37, May 1, 1909, 1). While there were apparently nothing in the articles with which Tomlinson and other leaders in the church would have disagreed, yet there were other teachings that they felt were necessary expressions of their faith and needed to be spelled out (e.g., footwashing, and certain ethical standards on marriage and holiness). Thereafter they became less ecumenical and more exclusive in their sectarian point of view. It became necessary, therefore, for the church to have its own paper.

[108]*General Assembly Minutes 1906-1914*, 77-79.

[109]The development of America's so-called social consciousness was occasioned by the Great Depression [1920s and early 1930s] and born with Franklin D. Roosevelt's "new deal" [1930s].

[110]This had developed out of Thomas Jefferson's philosophy of politics and government; see Phillips, "The Church of God: A Portrait of America," for the way this served as a context in the early development of the Church of God.

[111]Tomlinson, **Diary,** July 1899-1902; *Samson's Foxes* 1900-1902; Phillips, **Corruption,** 20-165.

[112]Ibid, March 10, 1901.

[113]*General Assembly Minutes 1906-1914*, 138; Mattie Perry advertized her school and home regularly in *The Bridegroom's Messenger*, 1907-1910.

[114]It is likely that this union failed for reasons similar to the attempt to form a union with the Mountain Assembly Church. In the case with the Mountain Assembly body it was made clear that the union was not a merger but a receiving of that body into the Church of God. Like her brother, Sam, Mattie was self-made and independent.

[115]*Minutes of the Fourteenth Annual Assembly*, 1919, 21.

[116]"Youth Interviews Experience," *The Lighted Pathway*, July 1949, 14.

[117]Spurling's license, written and endorsed by his father, stated, "That R. G. Spurling is ordained to the office of a Bishop . . . to do all the work that may devolve on him as a minister of the gospil [*sic*] being found sound in the Faith

bleaving [*sic*] in the general atonment [*sic*] and Resurrection of the Dead by our Lord Jesus Christ" (Xerox copy, WHPC).

[118]**Lost Link,** 11.

[119]Ibid, 11-12, and note poem, 38-39.

[120]Dr. Conn made this assessment (**Like A Mighty Army,** 21) and is probably correct. It should be remembered also that **The Lost Link** was written in 1897 with corrections and a supplement added between 1897 and the time the book was published in 1920.

[121]Ibid, 45.

[122]Spurling maintained that the mode of baptism should be left to an individual's conscience, though he himself favored "dipping" [*The Lost Link* (Original Manuscript), 12, 20]. The term, "immersion," was not acceptable in 1911 because it was not a biblical word. But the meaning was accepted, i.e., "that baptism is to plunge or dip, or a buriel [sic] beneath the water and lifting out again, and not sprinkling or pouring" (*General Assembly Minutes 1906-1914*, 86-87).

[123]**Lost Link,** 45.

[124]Ibid. Love was, in fact, "the lost link" through which to restore the New Testament church (Ibid, 9-10).

[125]Ibid.

[126]This may be seen by a casual reading of the Assembly minutes and by Tomlinson's messages in *The Bridegroom's Messenger* (1908- 1909). See note 107.

[127]Tomlinson made the practice of divine healing (actually faith healing) almost a test of fellowship. He even questioned a person's testimony of salvation if he/she used medicine. See Homer, **Diary,** Vol. 3, July 2, 1897; **Conflict,** 92-103; Phillips, **Corruption,** 30- 50.

[128]These teachings were already expressions of G. B. Cashwell, J. H. King, and the earliest Pentecostal leaders (see *The Bridegroom's Messenger* 1907-1910). Doubtlessly Church of God ministers borrowed the expressions from them; yet the doctrine of the church itself came to be interpreted differently by Church of God ministers, and this occasioned a slightly different twist on the interpretation of charismatic gifts.

[129]Tobacco habits were denounced by some (particularly by Tomlinson and Lemons) but tolerated in general until about 1908. See *General Assembly Minutes 1906-1914*,

11-13, 48-49, 60-61, 90-91. It is almost certain that Spurling did not denounce the use of tobacco. Its use was not prevented by the 1886 or 1895 covenants of Christian Union, which left the decision to the individual's "christianized conscience." There is testimony that John Paul Plemons, a charter member of Christian Union in 1886, used tobacco [testimony of his grandaughter], and at least two of R. G.Spurling's sons used tobacco.

[130]Ibid, 86-89. Spurling did not believe that tithing could be proven by the New Testament. (It should be remembered that this doctrine was rather new and strange in America and particularly in the Appalachian Mountains early in the twentieth century). He felt so strongly about this that he considered it a barrier to reuniting with Tomlinson and his followers in 1931. And, doubtlessly, he would not have reunited if Tomlinson would have made it a test of his ministry; but Tomlinson did not, and in fact reinstated him in the church as a bishop in 1931. These things have come to light recently by the discovery of letters of correspondence between Spurling and Tomlinson (Tomlinson to Spurling, October 29, 1930, December 6, 1930, January 13, 1931; Spurling to Tomlinson December 2, 1930, December 1, 1931, November 6, 1932, WHPC).

[131]*The Evening Light and Church of God Evangel*, August 15, 1910.

[132]*Minutes of the Eleventh Annual Assembly*, 1915, 33.

[133]The issue was first brought up in the Assembly in 1908 (*General Assembly Minutes 1906-1914*, 44-47). Differences over the meaning of "fornication" as it is used in Matthew 5:32 were argued passionately; and factions developed that at one point nearly divided the church. Tomlinson reflected upon the history of this development in his annual address in 1922, which gives insight that cannot be found elsewhere (**Historical Annual Addresses,** Vol.1, 192-194).

[134]*Minutes of the Thirteenth Annual Assembly*, 1917, 4-9; and see A. J. Tomlinson, "The Awful War," *Evangel*, February, 24, 1917; "The Awful War Seems Near," *Evangel*, March 31, 1917; "Days of Perplexity," *Evangel*, January 26, 1918. The reformation led by J. L. Scott—"The Original Church of God"—maintained this teaching after they broke away in 1919-1920 (*Minutes of the Convention of The Original Church of God*, June 19, 1920; WHPC). See also Mickey

Crews, **The Church of God: A Social History** (Knoxville: University of Tennessee Press, 1990), 108-137; Ann Elizabeth Murray, "Days of Perplexity: World War I and the Church of God," paper presented to University of Tennessee at Chattanooga, May 24, 1982, as partial fulfillment of bachelor's degree.

[135]During the selection of the General Overseer in November 1913, J. W. Buckalew remarked that "Reports have gone out that Brother Tomlinson has put himself in this place to rule over us" (*General Assembly Minutes 1906-1914*, 265).

[136]Tomlinson noted in his annual address in 1915, "I wish it to be distinctly understood now and forever that your General Overseer is a servant of God . . . and not a despotic ruler" (Ibid, 47). This explanation was occasioned evidently by some who understood his annual addresses to be dictatorial rather than suggestive (Ibid).

Again in his 1922 annual address Tomlinson noted that some counseled him to share the responsibilty of appointing members to the Council of Elders "in order to save the General Overseer certain criticism and accusations then going the rounds . . . "(Ibid, 207).

[137]*Minutes of the Thirteenth Annual Assembly*, 275-276.

[138]**Historical Annual Addresses**, Vol.1, 206-208.

[139]Ibid.

[140]*Minutes of the Fifteenth Annual Assembly*, 1920, 19.

[141]This was Tomlinson's position in his annual address in 1919 under the subtitle, "Equal Distribution," **Historical Annual Addresses**, Vol. 1, 107; he apparently had conceived the idea as early as 1916 [Ibid, 64-77], but in 1920 he spoke of it more in terms of an incentive plan according to the ministers' "needs and the efficiency of their work, and the responsibility of the position in which they serve" (Ibid, 135).

[142]Tomlinson acknowledged in his **Dairy** [September 2, 1921] that he had personally distributed the tithes "since January."

[143]**Like A Mighty Army**, 159-160.

[144]Ibid, 161-162.

[145]Tomlinson's actions did not impact the church until later in the year, and particularly at the Assembly in 1921.

[146]E. L. Simmons, **History of the Church of God** (Cleveland, TN: Church of God Publishing House, 1938), 38.

[147]So did F. J. Lee and other members of the Elders' Council.

[148]Llewellyn was a businessman and thought in terms of secular business more than pastoral. Tomlinson was the opposite, and this difference caused Llewellyn to develop a disdain for Tomlinson's leadership. Reports from several witnesses purported that Llewellyn and J. B. Ellis were by 1922 circulating negative reports about Tomlinson, and suggesting that the church needed a new General Overseer.

[149]"1)We do not believe in any man being the head of the Church of God; 2) We do not believe in State overseers, District overseers, nor overseers over tens, as they now have them in each local church as Governors, bosses or rulers of the Church of God; 3) We do not believe in the Elders as they have them to enforce their new laws and governments . . . 4) We do not believe in the late form of appointing pastors, but . . . the old form of each church selecting and calling its own pastor . . . " *Minutes of the Convention of The Original Church of God*, June 19, 1920, 7-8.

[150]*Minutes of the Convention of The Original Church of God*, June 19, 1920, Ridgedale, Tennessee, 4-5. Note the 16th teaching: "Tithing is voluntary. We stand on the original way of paying tithes, as on the other questions, doctrines, etc. Each member should pay tithes into the local treasury where they hold their membership. Deacons shall have charge of the tithe treasure . . . The pastor's need shall be supplied first . . . and the remaining tithes shall belong to the local church in which they are paid, and will be at the disposal of the said church" (Ibid). "We object to one-tenth of all tithes being sent to so-called HEAD QUARTERS . . . We also object to the remaining tithes left in the treasury, after the pastor is supplied, BELONGING to Head Quarters" (Ibid, 8).

[151]Perry had been called to account on some indiscretion by the Elders' Council. Lee noted that "We dealt with Perry for much less than what Tomlinson has done" (Letter from Lee to S. O. Gillaspie shortly after the June Council in 1923 [WHPC]). This disciplinary action doubtlessly influenced Perry's move.

[152]Spurling apparently turned in his license to Tomlinson after the Assembly in 1920 (for he had been listed consistently as a bishop in the Assembly minutes until 1920); and thereafter joined Scott's group in 1922 (Letter to Tomlinson, December 1, 1931 [WHPC]; and R. G. Spurling's *Certificate*

of Ordination signed by Scott in 1922 with the official seal of The Original Church of God [WHPC]).

Tomlinson's great admiration and deep affection for Spurling would not allow him apparently to revoke his license on the grounds of his complaint. Spurling had been offended because he had not been allowed to sell his newly published **The Lost Link** in the 1920 Assembly (letters from Spurling to Tomlinson, December 1, 1931, and Tomlinson to Spurling, January 13, 1931, WHPC). Thus Tomlinson probably held his license in his personal care, hoping that Spurling's hurt would heal, and that he would be reconciled. Meanwhile the church divided on a large scale in 1923. It is likely the "ten elders" faction of the broken body were unaware that Spurling had turned in his license to Tomlinson, and thus Lee [General Overseer] and Jernigan [pastor of Copper Hill, Tennessee, where Spurling's membership was] assumed he was a minister in the church, and acted accordingly. (Letter from F. J. Lee to John C. Jernigan, June 16, 1925; and see Phillips, "Transformed Tomlinson," 28-29).

[153]The charges were "1) J. S. Llewellyn is not in fellowship nor good standing with the church; 2) Disloyal as a member and bishop; 3) Guilty of lying; 4) Manifest a bad spirit at times; 5) Does not fill the requirements for a bishop . . . He is greedy of 'filthy lucre'!; He is not 'patient' in his home and with other people; "his notoriety as a 'brawler!"; He does not have a 'good report' of them which are without or within." These charges were quite evidently solid. The pastor, M. W. Letsinger, was a prominent and highly-esteemed minister in the church [thereafter was appointed as editor of the *Evangel*]. The charges were also signed by a bishop, deacon, evangelist, the clerk, J. M. Scarbrough, and two others [WHPC].

[154]Besides the evidence represented in the charges at the Chandlers View church [see notes 148, 153], M. W. Letsinger gave further witness that Llewellyn was basically dishonest [Testimony, WHPC]; F. J. Lee admitted that "Llewellyn was hard" and used "ridged terms," but excused him on the grounds of the nature of the investigation (Letter from Lee to Tomlinson, December 28, 1922 [WHPC]). W. M. Freels, the deacon of the Chandlers View church when charges had been brought against Llewellyn in 1916, later wrote [August 28,1924] to Tomlinson that he

had been warned of this "evil-doer" and that he was the "master mind" of the church's tragedy [WHPC].

[155]"The record shows that Mr. Llewellyn did not hestitate to combine business with religion, much to the profit of his business" ["Opinion," *Church of God vs. A.J. Tomlinson, Bradley Chancery*, July 13, 1925, 9]. The court's report goes on to show several transactions by Llewellyn through the church to his own profit [Ibid.] Another report says, "J. S. Llewellyn wanted A. J. Tomlinson to let him start a merchandise business—'with THE CHURCH OF GOD MEMBERS AS HIS SPECIAL CUSTOMERS.' A. J. Tomlinson turned him down FLAT, with the statement that 'The Church of God shall not be commercialized to any persons [*sic*] advantage'" (J. S. Llewellyn File [WHPC]).

[156]A. J. Tomlinson, "If You Only Knew The Truth," Church of God Bureau of Information, Cleveland, TN, November 10, 1923; J. P. Hughes, "Truth Against Fallacy," (CGBI); A. J. Lawson, Letter to Brother Richard, July 17, 1923; A. J. Lawson, "Charges," (CGBI), [WHPC].

[157]Bryant noted on one occasion, "When A. J. Tomlinson went into anything he had to be the head. I have been acquainted with [him] for a long time" (Bryant & Lemons interview, Document 27-A, 10). It is clear, however, that Bryant once held Tomlinson's leadership in high esteem. Tomlinson's influence on Bryant was so great that Bryant followed him to Cleveland, uprooting his long family tradition in the mountains to work with the man who apparently had the vision for world conquest and the future of the Church of God. Bryant became disgruntled after his prominence in leadership began to fade in 1917. He was not appointed to the newly created Council of Elders, and that same year for the first time was not re-appointed to oversee a state. The reasons for this are fairly clear. He was almost illiterate and was not especially gifted as a speaker. By 1917 his limitations could no longer meet the growing demands on leadership in the church. Requests to Tomlinson's office for Bryant's ministry fell off to nothing, and, in fact, many asked specifically that he not be appointed or assigned to their field of labor [Homer, **Diary,** Vol.2,34-35]. Tomlinson kept these things from Bryant, to avoid hurting him. This made it seem that Tomlinson had something against him, or in Bryant's words, "When the Church of God was small and requests would come in for ministers [Tomlinson]

would send me, and I would go. Now that the church is big . . . he don't send me any more. I was good enough then, but I ain't good enough now" [Ibid, 34]. The situation doubtlessly influenced his opposition to Tomlinson in the early 1920s. Perhaps more could have been done to honor his great pioneer spirit and contribution to the early development of the church, but at that stage in the church's short history there had not developed an appreciation for the church's early pioneers.

[158]Bryant & Lemons, 15-16; *The Bridegroom's Messenger* carried reports of the revival in Birmingham (December 1, 1907; January 1, 1908).

[159]*General Assembly Minutes 1906-1914*, 235.

[160]Lemons threatened Tomlinson and others with imprisonment and railed against them at the Assembly and in the June Council in 1923 (Letter from C. T. Anderson to F. J. Lee, December 16, 1922); C. T. Anderson, "Charges," June, 1923; Tomlinson, **Diary,** February 19, 1923. These actions were doubtlessly inspired in part by Llewellyn's influence. Lemons later made restitution to Tomlinson for his threats and for initiating the lawsuit (Tomlinson, **Diary,** August 13, 1930). We have no reason to doubt these reports by three witnesses, though a bias may have colored them in Tomlinson's favor.

[161]F. J. Lee had been in the middle of the road until after the Assembly in 1922. Tomlinson acknowledged that he did not know where Lee stood between the factions. Lee wrote to Gillaspie that "You know I was once teeth and toe nail with him [Tomlinson], but I tell you I was made to see things differently" (June 1923, [WHPC]).

[162]In a letter to Mrs. Addie Hunter explaining the circumstances of the division in 1922-1923, Lee stated, "We do not want to be bound by Satan nor by a pope [one man rule]..." (May 1, 1926, [WHPC].

[163]Tomlinson, **Diary,** February 19, 1923.

[164]Tomlinson had continually exalted the office of General Overseer since 1913. In his annual address in 1922 he spoke of it "in high and ennobling terms" because of the "grandeur and sacredness of the new position" (**Historical Annual Addresses,** Vol.1, 201-202). He also antagonized those who disagreed with the structure of the office, saying, "The enemy has had his machine guns aimed at this position for years" (Ibid, 201).

[165]*Call Council*, August 8-10, 1923, 7; "Opinion," *Church of God vs. A. J. Tomlinson, et al.*, Chancery Court, July 3, 1925, 1-9.

[166]This was admitted in the *Call Council*, 1923, 17. Tomlinson had noted in his **Diary** [September 2, 1921] that he was filling the office of General Overseer, of Editor and Publisher, of Publishing House Business Manager, of Superintendent of the Orphanage and Children's Home, and that he was working about 18 hours a day.

[167]*Minutes of the Sixteenth Annual Assembly*, 1921.

[168]Tomlinson came out boldly against the Constitution in his annual address in 1922, and called for its immediate abrogation (**Historical Annual Addresses,** Vol. 1, 197-199).

[169]*Call Council*, 7.

[170]The Committee on Order in the 1916 Assembly at first suggested that the General Overseer appoint the entire Council; but some took issue with that form of selection. The Committee reconsidered and brought back a recommendation that the General Overseer appoint two members and the three together appoint the remaining ten [*Minutes of the Twelfth Annual Assembly*, 1916, 32]. Tomlinson questioned the Committee's report and asked them to give reasons for the change. The Committee explained that they believed it was more in line with Bible order [Ibid]. Upon this explanation the power of God fell upon the Assembly, and it was said, "This seemed good to the Holy Ghost and us" [Ibid]. Tomlinson submitted, but obviously disagreed with the decision. His explanation in his annual address in 1922 [**Historical Annual Addresses,** Vol. 1, 206-208] in reference to the 1916 report is not consistent with the Minute of that Assembly [e.g., he denies that it was Scriptural and that "it seemed good to the Holy Ghost and us"]; and thus it seems to have reflected more his personal point of view at that time rather than the Assembly's.

[171]**Historical Annual Addresses,** Vol. 1, 206-208.

[172]Ibid, 202-203.

[173]Ibid, 198.

[174]*Minutes of the Seventeenth Annual Assembly*, 1922, "Report on Better Government," 48-50, and take note particularly of Llewellyn's amendments.

[175]Ibid.

[176]This was clearly established by Articles 1 [Purpose of

Organization] and 4 [Officers] in the Constitution with its amendents in 1922.

[177]Llewellyn admitted to the incident in court, but explained that "the flourish of his hand was only a gesture and that he complained because Tomlinson would not recognize the speakers in favor of the amendment" ("Opinion," *Church of God vs. A.J. Tomlinson, et al.*, Bradley Chancery, July 3, 1925, 4).

[178]Ibid. Some felt, however, that the measure had been forced to a conclusion.

[179]*Minutes of the Seventeenth Annual Assembly*, 1922, 52.

[180]Ibid; and "Opinion," 4.

[181]A. J. Lawson was one of Tomlinson's greatest admirers and remained true to him to the end; but admitted "that Brother Tomlinson made many mistakes" (Letter to T. A. Richard, July 17, 1923).

[182]It is true that most of the leaders approved of Tomlinson in 1913-1914; but it is not likely that they fully understood the office as Tomlinson understood it. The position was new and developing. In any case, they felt that they had a perfect right and obligation to change their opinion regarding the powers of the office, particularly as it developed and was practiced by Tomlinson.

[183]"Many of the ministers were so disturbed and discouraged because of the measures passed by the influence of these men, and the way the Assembly ended, that many of them could not go to their respective fields of labor with any degree of victory and joy, to toil and labor for the Church of God...while such men [were] allowed to be in control" (*Charges*, 2-3).

[184]This was brought out clearly in court. "Opinion," *Church of God vs. A. J. Tomlinson, et al.*, 3-4.

[185]Ibid, 4.

[186]Lee's letter to Tomlinson [April 13, 1923] describes these incidents during the Council meeting [WHPC].

[187]"Opinion," *Church of God vs. A. J. Tomlinson, et al.*, 4.

[188]The alternative, of course, was for Tomlinson to have acted with the Council of Twelve and the Committee that was to have been appointed to oversee the distribution of the tithes.

[189]This was against Tomlinson's will and judgment. He had at first appointed the Committee but Lewellyn objected on grounds that it unreasonable for a man to appoint a committee to investigate himself ["Opinion," *Church of God vs. A. J. Tomlinson, et al.*, 4]. Thus the Elders' Council made

the appointments and added Llewellyn to the two whom Tomlinson had formerly appointed (Ibid).

[190]This committee was appointed on September 5, 1922.

[191]He had said on more than one occasion that he was "more or less subject to the Assembly" (e.g, "Introduction" to his annual address in 1915) but he evidently meant "less." The actions in 1921-1923 prove this, for the Assembly approved the Constitution which Tomlinson refused to live under after 1922. Evidence is everywhere in his own writings that he felt that the office of General Overseer was above the Assembly, and he practiced the government of the church on that principle. The notion that the General Overseer was subject to the General Assembly was superficial, because the Assembly was more or less a faceless body in regard to holding the General Overseer accountable. This was in part the reason for the creation of the Council of Elders [See Phillips, "Transformed Tomlinson," 12-20].

[192]There are too many witnesses against "reasonable doubt" that Llewellyn was manuevering to remove Tomlinson from office. *Call Council,* 22.

[193]The audit was made by the Lee H. Battle Audit Company of Chattanooga. This "preliminary examination" clearly admits that the report is incomplete, made without availibility of several "day books or cash books" and that "a complete audit would require many weeks of hard work" (Report from Lee H. Battle Company to Messrs. J. S. Llewellyn, F. J. Lee, J. B. Ellis, Finance Committee, April 12, 1923 [WHPC]). It is curious that Lee insisted that the audit was complete in view of what the auditors themselves admitted.

[194]Tomlinson was in the Bahamas and Florida during the commission of the audit. Neither he nor his bookkeeper, Lillie Duggar, were consulted during the audit. If books were missing, they could have been summoned upon request. Llewellyn was the principal person dealing with the audit company, and took the responsibility of supplying the auditors with what they needed. Tomlinson was doubtlessly correct in assuming, "I do not consider that this Auditor's report is unbiased. I mean by this that there is a streak of somebody's (J. S. Lewellyn's) influence all the way through it" (Tomlinson, "Personal Notes" regarding the Council and Auditor's Report, 11. k., [WHPC]).

[195]In a letter written to Tomlinson on Christmas Day in 1922, Lee was still respectful, but evidently no longer awed by

Tomlinson's position or personal influence over him. He pointed out several things that particularly disturbed him, including the fact that Tomlinson had the *Faithful Standard* copyrighted in his own name, which thing Lee had kept quite to "hold down further strife" (WHPC). The day following the auditor's report, however, Lee wrote Tomlinson a more firm letter, reprimanding him, and warning that he was "laying traps for [himself] in the Federal courts." Lee fully accepted the audit as complete, noting that the evidence against Tomlinson "shows up very serious" (April 13, 1923 [WHPC]). Lee wrote to S. O. Gillaspie after the June Council, "You know I was teeth and toe nail with him [Tomlinson], but I tell you I was made to see things differently." He went on to say that he could not "cover up the things [I] know about him just because of sympathy and his smooth way of expressing himself without being held accountable to God (WHPC)." The fact that Tomlinson reported to the Assembly that the *Faithful Standard* had earned only 60 dollars for the year but later admitted that it had earned 200 dollars per month, greatly influenced Lee's opinion against Tomlinson's integrity [though the court attributed this discrepancy to "one of [Tomlinson's] exaggerating promoting ideas not based upon the facts" ["Opinion,"9]. Reports [as early as February] that Tomlinson was planning to divide the Church and start over to re-establish his position affected Lee's opinion of him. The reports were doubtlessly true, and for this reason Homer says his father started over again in February 1923 [**Diary**, Vol.2, 23-25].

[196]Boehmer wrote to J. A. Davis, "Bro. Davis there has been lots said about Bro. Tomlinson that is untrue. We thought Bro. Tomlinson had taken Church of God money to pay his own debts, but we have found out better. We found his own checkbook here where he had paid his own bills out . . . and there is lots of other things coming to light the same way. This is a bad thing and somebody is going to die over this. I hardly know what to do some times. I love Bro. Tomlinson and hate to take a stand against him, but if I stand with him I will loose my job, and I have got a good job which you know, so I hardly know what to do. Now Bro. Davis dont let no body [sic] know what I have wrote [sic] you" (WHPC).

[197]An opinion offered to the writer in 1983 should be submitted here into evidence as part of the testimony of the case,

since the person who made it lived and worked in Cleveland during the whole ordeal of the 1920s, and he knew all the leaders of both factions. J. R. Kinser, former General Treasurer for the Church of God of Prophecy, had worked at the Church of God Publishing House since 1920. He considered Lee a good man but believed he had become influenced by opinions that he himself should be the General Overseer.

[198]This campaign was institutionalized after the disruption and went by the name, "Bureau of Information," managed by A. J. Lawson. Pamphlets were printed that contained testimonies and explanations that contradicted the "ten elders" faction's interpretation of the reasons for the disruption. Letters from C. T. Anderson and Lawson's tract, *Charges*, clearly show Tomlinson's encouragement to publish contradictions of the controversy. This was born at the 1922 Assembly in the heart C. T. Anderson (Ibid).

[199]Tomlinson devoted a whole section of his annual address to "Wirepulling," feeling that it was his "duty to leave the warning on record" (**Historical Annual Addresses,** Vol. 1, 204-205). C. T. Anderson wrote that "M. S. Lemons, J. S. Llewellyn and J. B. Ellis were most prominent by their wire pulling and chicanery . . . J. S. Llewellyn in a discourse of two hours or more . . . used such words and terms in trying to ruin the influence of the General Overseer and his family . . . that were unbecoming for...a political trickster . . . and by open and boisterous discourses said Lemons, Ellis, and Llewellyn have proven themselves to be brawlers and contentious"(*Charges*, 2).

[200]C. T. Anderson had written up charges against Lemons, Llewellyn, and Ellis, following the Assembly in 1922 and expected to present them at the next scheduled Council of Elders. When the meeting was called on June 12 he presented them to the Council. He was joined with comments by others including Brouayer that held the floor for about two hours. Some of the Elders felt that this was a scheme planned to preempt the primary purpose for the meeting, which was to hear Tomlinson's explanation of the auditor's report that showed the $14,141.83 shortage. It was finally agreed to set aside the charges against Lemons, Llewellyn and Ellis, until the business with Tomlinson was concluded (T. S. Payne promised that he would make sure that the charges against the three elders would be pursued later, though they never were [Tomlinson, **Diary,** September 10,

1923]). Tomlinson's explanation was unsatisfactory to most of the remaining Elders (Lee wrote later that he was "like a drowning man grabbing at a straw" [Lee to Gillaspie, July, 1923, WHPC]. This was followed by several comments and a tirade of arguments by Llewellyn, who railed against Tomlinson and his family, and insisted that the General Overseer step down from the chair due to the nature of the business involving him. This was argued in confusion and near mayhem for some time. Tomlinson finally agreed [reluctantly] to give up the chair, but before leaving he related a story that he felt was appropriate for the situation. "I gave them a story about an old mule that had fallen into a well and the owner decided that since he was not worth the cost of getting him out he would fill up the well and let the mule stay in the bottom thereof. Accordingly he began to dump rocks and earth in on top of the mule, and he shook it off and got on top of it until he finally walked out at the top and began grazing as if nothing had ever happened. I told them to go ahead and cover me up and bruise me all they could, and in due time I would walk out at the top and go on grazing as if nothing had ever happened" (**Answering the Call,** 22- 23). Efford Haynes was chosen to chair the meeting thereafter. The meeting continued in Tomlinson's absence evidently in an effort to persaude Gillaspie and Brouayer against Tomlinson, in order to gain a consensus. When this failed the "ten elders" met separately and filed their charges against Tomlinson, Gillaspie, and Brouayer. Besides the original documents presented, see cross opinions in **Like A Mighty Army,**175-180 and **Upon This Rock,** 573-646; see also Duggar, **A. J. Tomlinson,** 194-216, and Tomlinson, **Diary,** February 19- September 10, 1923.

[201]Ibid.

[202]In 1920 a "Declaration" was made by the Assembly that legally incorporated the local churches as part of the General Assembly of the Church of God. This was evidently set up by the General Overseer's call for "Identification" in his annual Address in order to bind the local churches and "to prevent troubles and disorders similar to some we have had in the past" [referring to J. L. Scott's reformation] (*Minutes of the Fifteenth Annual Assembly,* 1920,23).

Thereafter the Constitution was adopted in 1921 and amended in 1922. The "Declaration" of Tomlinson and his followers on June 27, 1923 was intended, therefore, to denounce these measures passed by the Assembly and called for a return to former practices before the Assembly's declaration was made in 1920. (The Declaration of Tomlinson and his followers was signed by Tomlinson, George T. Brouayer, S. O. Gillaspie, H. A. Pressgrove, J. F. Dover, and A. J. Lawson; WHPC. Scores of copies were printed with blank sheets at the end to solicit signatures for petition against the Assembly resolutions adopted 1920-1922.

[203]It was considered duly called because the General Overseer had called it according to established practice [and even according to the Constitution, Article 4, Section 6], and orderly because Gillaspie, Brouayer, and Tomlinson formed a quorum of the Council. The "ten elders" denied the orderliness of the meeting on grounds that they had agreed among themselves in Council that at least nine were required to make a quorum, and that they were not given adequate notification. Tomlinson, Gillaspie, and Brouayer maintained, however, that the "ten elders" had been notified properly and simply boycotted the meeting.

[204]This was a foregone conclusion since Llewellyn, Lemons, Ellis, Lee, and McLain were five of the Judges. E. J. Boehmer and S. W. Latimer were the other two. They had been appointed in the Seventeenth Annual Assembly (see *Minutes of the Seventeenth Annual Assembly*, 1922, 106).

[205]*Call Council*, 1-24. In reflecting on the Call Council three months later in his annual address in November 1923, he said, "In this conference it was acknowledged that the constitution just as literally destroyed the Church of God as the Nicene Creed destroyed it in the year 325, and the only thing left for us to do was repudiate the constitution and...resolve ourselves back into the Church of God under Bible rule and government" [**Historical Annual Addresses,** Vol.1, 219].

[206]His analogy about the "old mule" in the "June Council" [**Answering the Call**, 22-23; and see note 200] was a perfect illustration of his prevailing disposition during and after the disruption. Ten years after the division [1933] he reflected on his ordeal and his "old mule" story and declared, "And this statement has been fully verified and realized."

[207]He was arrested and fined at least eight times for refusing to comply with court rulings in regard to the use of the

name, Church of God. This was a sacred name to Tomlinson and his followers [see Questions and Subjects Committee's report to the Assembly, September 14, 1929 in regard to the name, Church of God], and they fully believed that it belonged to them by a divine decree higher than the courts of men. Others [e.g., A. J. Lawson and A. D. Evans] were arrested and fined with Tomlinson on occasion for representing themselves as the Church of God. When asked at the Call Council in August 1923 if a letter were addressed to The Church of God, Cleveland, Tennessee, who would get it? Tomlinson declared, "I would. I have received this mail and shall continue. We are the Church of God. We have not drawn out out as they would have you believe, but they have gone out" [*Call Council*, 7-8]. This remained his consistent opinion in the face of court rulings and public criticism.

[208]Lawson was left in charge of its construction, while Tomlinson hit the field evangelizing and re-gathering what he could of the sheep scattered during the "confusion and deception." Tomlinson described the crude structure erected in such a hurry to accomodate the 1923 Assembly in his annual address in 1924, and reflected upon the victory and enthusiasm manifested by those who attended ["The Tabernacle," **Historical Annual Addresses,**Vol.1, 235-236]. See also *The White Wing Messenger*, October 13, 1923 for details of the purchase of the property on Central Avenue and open air services.

[209]*Call Council*, 23-24.

[210]*Minutes of the Eighteenth Annual Assembly*, 16.

[211]Tomlinson traveled and evangelized extensively for several years after starting over. While he was away, A. J. Lawson [1869-1948] was indispensable in holding things together in Cleveland. Lawson was a capable deacon and businessman and rendered invaluable service to the church until he died in 1948. Gillaspie and Brouayer were also instrumental, especially Gillaspie [Brouayer died in April 1929]; and Tomlinson's son, Homer, his daughter, Iris, and son-in-law, Avery D. Evans, were all dedicated to rebuilding the church under the oversight of Tomlinson.

[212]He drew parallels frequently between the history of the Church of God and America in his messages and annual addresses, particularly after the division in 1923. He made references to the Civil War and Reconstruction Periods in

particular. See, e.g., his annual address in 1928, note particularly the section subtitled, "Problems In Reconstruction" [**Historical Annual Addresses,** Vol.2, 14-15].

[213]The depression in the 1920s was occasioned by the rapid expansion of business before and during World War I. Farmers had bought more land and machinery because of the momentary demand occasioned by the war. However, after the war the demand fell off and markets collasped, particularly for farmers in the mid-west and cotton farmers in the South. The circumstances were even worse in Appalachia where the majority of Tomlinson's followers congregated in the 1920s.

[214]Note the sections subtitled, "Helps and Governments" and "Our Big Business Program," in his annual address in 1928 [**Historical Annual Addresses,** Vol. 2, 32-42. This was the beginning of the development of an elaborate and complex system of organization that funneled funds to an ever-burgeoning headquarters in Cleveland.

[215]The church assumed about a twelve thousand dollar indebtedness, though Baney and the other donors did not require it [see "Resolution of Appreciation for Orphanage Gift" presented to the Twenty-Third Annual Assembly, September 17, 1928].

[216]First of all, Richard G. Spurling considered Christian Union to be the restoration of the New Testament church, which Tomlinson acknowledged to be the Church of God. This was stated in the covenant of Christian Union. They "agreed to set [sic] together as the Church of God to transact business . . ." [**Conflict**, 207], and Richard Spurling dedicated "the infant church of God" [Ibid, 208]. Secondly, Tomlinson acknowledged Richard Spurling to be the first ordained minister in the restored Church of God, and credited him with "assisting to launch this last great reformation that is now assuming such vast proportions . . ." [Ibid]. Thirdly, he claimed Christian Union to be the "infant organization" [Ibid, 209] that found continuity in the Holiness Church at Camp Creek in 1902 [Ibid, 213]. Fourthly, he clearly acknowledged that he "joined with the faithful little flock to push the work along" [Ibid, 214]; and that he and two deacons on June 13, 1903 "were ordained by the church in proper order" [Ibid]. He states that when he joined the church a more careful study of the New Testament order had been made [at least on his own part],

but the result of this was only "that the work revived and took upon it a new impetus" [Ibid]. Even in 1928 he acknowledged that he had joined the church which was already in existence; and that the Church of God in 1928 was a continuation of the Holiness Church at Camp Creek which had been organized with sixteen members [**Historical Annual Addresses,** Vol. 2, 13]. Tomlinson's entire historical narrative endeavors to maintain a continuous action of the church from 1886 to 1903 [**Conflict,** 205- 216].

[217]By 1941 he had completely revised the interpretation of his experience when he joined the church. During a special program in Fields of the Wood on September 7, 1941, he reflected on the day he joined the church, and noted, "Right here I gave my hand to Brother Spurling, who was not a Church of God member exactly like we are, but he and others were spiritually good. But they never brought us up and said we are the Church of God. I said it myself, and because I said it God has been honoring it ever since. You are all Church of God because I am" (*Minutes of Fields of the Wood Programs* [WHPC]; A. J. Tomlinson, **God's Anointed—Prophet of Wisdom** [Cleveland, TN: WWPH, 1943],13; Duggar, **Tomlinson,** 665-669. This ambiguous statement reveals the development of his new interpretation of the church's origins. After 1923 he began to reflect more and more upon his early association with Spurling, Bryant, and the saints in the Holiness Church at Camp Creek, and particularly the day he joined the church in 1903. Before he joined the church he had apparently taken issue [or thought he had] with Spurling on a particular point regarding the nature of the church. Spurling interpreted Jesus' declaration—"I will build my church"— as a dynamic process rather than a static point in history. He maintained that the church was real and visible, yet something always-in-the-making. "If Christ built a church, when did he finish it? Not yet, I assure you, or He would come and receive it. Like the temple of old it was not built in a day or a year. So is the heavenly Jerusalem, the bride, every saint is a stone in the temple of God. Rev. 3:12. Thank God that you and I may be a part of God's church. Built by Christ—yes, here on earth is God's quarry and every stone that does not spoil in dressing, in the quarry [visible church] will, when perfected through suffering like

Jesus was, fit perfectly in the church triumphant—the temple of God. So the church is being built" [Lost Link, 18-19]. He maintained this view in his message to the Eighth Assembly in 1913: "On the day of Pentecost [Christ] laid the foundation of the church and it is still in process of construction" [*General Assembly Minutes 1906- 1914*, 195]. This evidently was the point that was discussed on June 13 to which Tomlinson's refers "we made a more careful study of the New Testament order," **Conflict,** 214] before he joined the church and with which he later took issue. In his annual address in 1928, he clearly denounced Spurling's view of the church and the premise upon which he joined it. "It has been insisted by many that the church started on the day of Pentecost [Tomlinson himself had maintained this view in 1912, **Conflict,** 154] and went on in its process of construction from that time. But I insist that that view is erroneous...The record does not state that the church was partly constructed and now He is adding more pieces toward its completion. It is rather stated that the house was up, and that it was a complete house, but now He is putting some additions to it—that is, increasing its membership" [**Historical Annual Addresses,** Vol.2, 16-17]. He went on to state that "Jesus had His church already built" and thus "the addition of more members did not make it any more complete than before..." [Ibid, 17]. It was about this time also that he changed his view on the relationship between the church and the bride. He had argued passionately for Spurling's view that the church in this present world was militant and through suffering would be perfected and become the bride in heaven [**Conflict,** 132-143]. He had maintained this view even in his annual address in 1926 [*Minutes of the Twenty-First Annual Assembly*, 49]. Thus in 1928, with Spurling and Bryant and the others no longer present and in fellowship with him, he began to revise the church's history from the standpoint of his personal experience on Burger Mountain, and the moot point that he had made regarding the nature of the church before he consented to join on June 13th. But he does not make this explicit until September 7, 1941: "Then I said, 'You have agreed that this that I have said makes it the Church of God, and will you be willing to take it and keep it the Church of God?' They said they were willing. I then asked if they were willing to take me in with the understanding that it IS the Church of God—not going to be, but IS the Church of God?" [**God's Anointed**, 12]. That Tomlinson at this late date embellished the story could be argued easily on the basis of his former testimonies that he knew nothing of the Church of God when he joined it. His historical accounts had always depicted himself as the student and Spurling as the teacher, particularly in the exchanges made on June 13, 1903. "I poured in the questions and Bible answers were given which satisfied all my inquiries. I then said, this means that it is the Church of God. To this they assented" [**Answering the Call,** 17]. Even if Tomlinson's version in 1941 was exactly as it happened in 1903, Spurling consented to take him into the church because he had maintained this point of view from the beginning— that it was indeed the Church of God [see note 209]. Tomlinson's statement, "This means that it is the Church of God" [Ibid] was later said to be an exclamation, "It IS the Church of God!" [**God's Anointed**, 7], but in either case Spurling and the Holiness Church at Camp Creek understood it to be an admission from Tomlinson rather than a new revelation for themselves. Explicating the name— Church of God—meant very little to Spurling [or to Tomlinson for that matter, **Conflict,** 215-216] for they believed Christian Union and the Holiness Church at Camp Creek were in actuality the Church of God. In point of fact, the explication of the name—Church of God—was not adopted until 1907, and it was suggested by H. L. Trim or M. S. Lemons, not Tomlinson [Bryant and Lemons interview, 6]. Tomlinson, in fact, did not maintain that the name "Church of God" was an exclusive designation for the Bible church [See **Conflict,** 215-216]. It may be that Tomlinson's static institutional concept of the church [which he later determined had been fulfilled on the day of its organization recorded in Mark 3:13-16] simply failed to comprehend Spurling's militant-triumphant eschatology of the church [**Lost Link** 17-18], and thus in later years [with Spurling in his grave and Bryant in another organization] he magnified the point that he had made on the day he joined the church in order to justify his new interpretation. But, doubtlessly, his later interpretation of Isaiah 60:1-8, which enabled him to identify 1903 as the year that this passage was fulfilled in connection with the airplane [v.8], overwhelmed all else. This notion came to him on June 16, 1939: ". . . I discovered today that the Wright Bros. made their first airplane flight of from 9 to 59 seconds in Dec. 1903. I joined the church on Camp Creek N.C. June 13, 1903. They in extreme eastern N. C. and I in extreme western N. C. This bit of information thrills me because of the prophecy of Isaiah 60-1,8 [Tomlinson, **Diary,** June 16, 1939]. Thus the moment he joined the church Isaiah 60:1 was fulfilled—"Arise, shine, for thy light is come"—which he had determined by retrospection. A few months later he noted in his Diary, "Also went over into N.C. and viewed the place where I was first taken into the church that afterward became the Church of God of Prophecy . . . I am planning to purchase a spot in north-east county of N.C. where the first airplane was constructed. These are taken to correspond with prophecy—Isaiah 60:1-8" [**Diary**, November 27, 1939]. He was then able to reinterpret many passages of Scripture as prophecies related to his experience on Burger Mountain, and his union with the church on June 13, 1903. This is explicated in his annual address in 1941 (**Historical Annual Addresses**, Vol.3), 193- 200, 215-222; and see his explanations made during the dedication of Fields of the Wood in September 1941 [**God's Anointed,** 7-12].

It may be seen that Tomlinson's revised interpretation of the church's restoration ruled out Spurling and Bryant, and all the ministers and members who had covenanted together to be the church before Tomlinson joined on June 13, 1903. In order to justify this new interpretation he says, "I gave my hand to Brother Spurling, who was not a Church of God member exactly like we are..." [**God Anointed**, 13]. This created an unexplainable ambiguity that actually contradicted the historical facts, for Spurling and Bryant had been considered faithful pillars in the church before Tomlinson joined. Neither was it necessary for them to renew their covenants or their licenses after June 13, 1903 in order to be a part of the church; for it was well understood by all that they were ministers in the church before Tomlinson, including Tomlinson himself. Indeed, it was Spurling who convinced the former Quaker of the nature of the visible church and his need to join it; and it was he who administered the covenant of membership to Tomlinson; and it was he who ordained him with the assistance of Bryant on June 13, 1903. Tomlinson admitted all these things in his eulogy of Spurling in the *White Wing Messenger* ["R. G. Spurling Passes Over the Tide," June 22, 1935, 1, 4]. His revision of the church's history came four years after Spurling's death. It is rather amazing that Tomlinson's followers did not question his revision of history until the late 1980s [See Phillips, "Transformed Tomlinson," 10-12].

[218] **Historical Annual Addresses**, Vol.2, 55.

[219] We cannot find an explicit statement in this regard until 1939 [Tomlinson, **Diary**, June 16, 1939; and see note 217]. The analogy of the tree, branches and "little unassuming bud" in **Conflict**, 155-159 is the only reference that comes even remotely close to suggesting what he later developed and mythologized. Everything else contradicts until 1939. But his experience on Burger Mountain in 1903 had become a growing myth after 1928. In 1941 Tomlinson explained, "When I climbed to the top of Burger Mountain on the morning of the thirteenth of June, 1903, to meet the Lord in prayer...and then returned to the base of the mountain and met with the brethren and sisters for the study of the Scriptures which resulted in the finding of the Church of God of the last days. The church of the Bible had been lost to view for more than a thousand years, but on that memorable day it made its appearance again in fulfillment of Scriptures" (**God's Anointed**, 7). A. D. Evans wrote, "On that memorable morning, June 13, 1903, while Brother Tomlinson knelt in prayer on the summit of Burger Mountain...the vision of the Church of God began to dawn upon him, and to take form. To that vision many revelations have been added, until today, literally hundreds of thousands owe their vision of the Church of God to this mighty Prophet of Wisdom [Ibid, "Introduction"]. No one did more to develop and embellish the myth about Burger Mountain and June 13, 1903 than Tomlinson's son, Homer [except Tomlinson himself]. "That name was revealed as being all-sufficient for the body of Christ on earth in a wonderful experience on Burger Mountain . . . June 13, 1903 . . . A. J. Tomlinson . . . came upon a single church located in the Fields of the Wood, at the foot of Burger Mountain, like Moses coming to the burning bush back of Mount Horeb (Sinai). Like Moses, he turned aside to see what it was. When God saw Moses turned aside to

investigate, He spoke to him. When A. J. Tomlinson turned aside to investigate, God spoke to him. Like Jacob, after the vision was revealed, he exclaimed in words that have proven prophetic by amazing evidences since in every nation of the world. Like John the Baptist in the wilderness of Judea, amidst the multitudes who came to be baptized he saw One...'and bare record that this is the Son of God'. . . Yes, in that same wonder came A. J. Tomlinson upon that church in the Fields of the Wood at the foot of Burger Mountain and said, on June 13, 1903, 'This is the Church of God!'" [Homer A. Tomlinson, "Weapons of Warfare," quoted in **God's Anointed**, "Introduction"]. And see notes 220-224. Tomlinson became more deeply convinced of his claims in regard to his Burger Mountain experience on June 13, 1903, after he was able to identify Isaiah 60:8 as the fulfillment of the Wright Brothers Kitty Hawk flight on December 17, 1903. Great claims were thus made about Isaiah 60:1-8 in regard to his experience on Burger Mountain and the Wright Brothers flight at Kitty Hawk in the same state [North Carolina] and year [1903]; [**Historical Annual Addresses,** Vol.3, 194-195, 215- 220; Tomlinson, **Diary,** June 16 and November 27, 1939]. This opened the door for more extravagant interpretations of passages in Isaiah 13-62. The display of the flag on a tree in Fields of the Wood was said to have fulfilled Isaiah 13:2 [**Historical Annual Addresses**, Vol.3,196]; a loud speaker fulfilled passages [Ibid, 197] such as "exalt the voice" [Isaiah 37:23] and "lift up the voice" [Isaiah 52:8]; the springs of water at the base of Burger Mountain fulfilled Isaiah 49:10; Tomlinson himself claimed to be "a man of prophecy" fulfilling Isaiah 66:2 and Jeremiah 30:21 [Ibid, 187; and **God's Anointed**, 8-9]; and many other passages were said to have been fulfilled when Tomlinson joined the church on June 13, 1903 [See his last four annual addresses 1939-1943, **Historical Annual Addresses**, Vol.3, 97-275; and see also note 217].

[220]This found its final form inscribed in concrete on the "MEMORIAL OF THE VISION" marker in Fields of the Wood: "...THE NEXT MORNING, JUNE 13, 1903, HE AROSE EARLY AND WAS LED BY THE SPIRIT TO THE TOP OF THIS MOUNTAIN, KNOWN TODAY AS PRAYER MOUNTAIN. THERE HE PRAYED AND PREVAILED UNTIL GOD GAVE HIM THE FIRST VISION OF THE CHURCH OF GOD OF THE

LAST DAYS, THUS FULFILLING JER. 30:21...HE LEFT THE MOUNTAIN TOP AND CAME DOWN TO THE HOUSE WHERE HE WAS IN A MEETING WITH A FEW MEMBERS OF A CHURCH THEN KNOWN AS THE HOLINESS CHURCH AT CAMP CREEK. THERE HE BECAME A MEMBER OF THE CHURCH WITH THE UNDERSTANDING THAT IT IS THE CHURCH OF GOD OF THE BIBLE...THIS MAKING HIM THE FIRST MEMBER TO JOIN THE LAST DAYS CHURCH OF GOD. THIS WAS THE BEGINNING OF THE FULFILLMENT OF ISA. 60:1..." [C.T. Davidson, **America's Unusual Spot** (Cleveland,TN: WWPH, 1954), 62-63].

[Note: this marker was reworded in 1995 to honor Christ, the head of the church. Other markers in Fields of the Wood have also been reworded to reflect the history of the church as it was written before the Burger Mountain tradition and revision in 1939].

[221]Nothing could show more vividly the extent to which the myth of June 13, 1903 had become entrenched after Tomlinson's death than the case of R. G. Spurling's son, Pinkney. In 1949 Pinkney, then a minister in Tennessee, challenged some of the ministers for preaching that "the Church of God had its beginning June 13, 1903" (Letter from M. A. Tomlinson to L. V. Jones, August 25, 1949, [WHPC]). When confronted by the state overseer of Tennessee, L. V. Jones, Pinkney maintained his contention and was charged by the overseer for disloyalty. On appeal to the General Overseer, the charge was upheld. Pinkney's license was revoked with the following explanation: "Ministry revoked August 24, 1949 for disloyalty to the church and denouncing its teachings. When approached by the presbytery, he showed a very bad spirit and stated that our preachers were preaching lies when they say the Church of God had its beginning June 13, 1903" [Ibid]. Jones' response to Tomlinson's decision expressed his grief over the situation but noted, "Regardless of the grief and suffering, I feel that we need loyal ministers" [L. V. Jones to M. A. Tomlinson, n.d].

[222]The details of the purchase of the land and early development of Fields of the Wood were carefully chronicled in Charles T. Davidson's first edition of **Fields of the Wood** (Cleveland, TN:WWPH, 1948). This book also magnified the mythological themes invented by A. J. Tomlinson and embellished by Homer A. Tomlinson, Grady R. Kent, and others.

223Ibid, 19-20.

224See notes 217, 219. Homer wrote prolifically between 1939-1944 of his father's Burger Mountain experience and its significance according to prophecy. He went to great lengths in "Mountain of the Lord's House" [1941] to compare Burger Mountain with Mt. Sinai and his father with Moses, employing his limited knowledge of the German language to make some extravagant claims about the terms, *burg* and *burger* [WHPC]. That same year he wrote, "There Shall Be Wings," endeavoring to show that his father's experience on Burger Mountain, June 13, 1903, and the Wright brothers flight at Kitty Hawk, North Carolina on December 17, 1903, together fulfilled Isaiah 60:1-8 [WHPC]. He published also several articles and stories in the *Joyful News* between 1939-1943, which further enhanced the growing tradition of Burger Mountain and June 13, 1903.

225Tomlinson, **Diary**, 1940-1943; Duggar, **Tomlinson,** 665-716; **Answering the Call**, 28-29.

226In his annual address in 1933 (**Historical Annual Addresses**, Vol.2, 190), he admits that he had been contemplating a flag for more than ten years. Later in 1939 he noted, "No other body of people can justly claim to be the last days church because no others came up with the flying machine in accord with prophecy. And the others who were once with me, and are not anymore, have surely lost their identity and claim. And by our having the flag of prophecy and they have not, that certainly finishes showing the chasm between" [**Historical Annual Addresses,** Vol.3, 128].

227Ibid, Vol.3, 48.

228Ibid, Vol.2, 191-192, 215-217.

229Ibid, 190.

230*Minutes of the Twenty-Eighth Annual Assembly,* 41-43.

231"The Banner of Love," **Hymns of Glorious Praise** (Springfield, MO: Gospel Publishing House, 1969), 530. This song was written by Clemmie P. McAnally and copyrighted in 1945 by WWHP.

232**Historical Annual Addresses**, Vol. 3, 128; and see note 217.

233Tomlinson encouraged this in his annual addresses beginning in 1934. Ibid, Vol. 2, 215-222; **Answering the Call,** 27-28.

[234]He wrote under the subtitle—"Our Mighty Flag"—in his 1939 annual address, "Only recently I have discovered new beauties and additional powers vested in the Flag." He went on to attribute almost magical powers to the flag in order to inspire loyalty and service to the church [**Historical Annual Addresses**, Vol.3, 108- 111]. In his annual address in 1935, he had noted "I think every member should have one [a flag] on the front porch or in a front window of their home as a sign of membership in the Church of God. It might be a protection some time or other means of blessing [Ibid, Vol.2, 249].

[235]"Flag worshipers," "Rag Worshipers," "Church idolaters," etc., were common accusations from those who had little sympathy for Tomlinson and his followers.

[236]A handbook was also published by the General Properties Committee in 1950 which outlined the meaning and purpose of the flag, and illustrated proper ways to display the flag on special occasions.

[237]See *White Wing Messenger*, August 29, September 26, November 7, December 19, 1936; *Cleveland Daily Banner*, September 12, 1936; *Minutes of the Thirty-First Annual Assembly*, 1936, 14-15; Homer A. Tomlinson, *Miracles of Healing In The Ministry of Rev. Francisco Olazabal* (Published by author, Queens, N.Y., 1939).

[238]Homer, **Diary,** Vol. 2, 69-74; *Ministry of Healing*, 1.

[239]Ibid; *Ministry of Healing*, 16-20; *Minutes of the Thirty-First Annual Assembly*, 1936, 15.

[240]"Hundreds Pray All Night At Unique Healing Service," *Cleveland Daily Banner*, September 12, 1936, 1.

[241]Homer, **Diary,** Vol. 2, 71-79.

[242]The story was carried in the *Cleveland Daily Banner*, September 1937; as well as the *White Wing Messenger*, "A Mighty Man of God Has Fallen In The Midst of His Labors," July 3, 1937, 1, 4.

[243]Homer Tomlinson was primarily responsible for the popularity of the Great Speckled Bird motif. He planned and directed special programs at Fields of the Wood and during the General Assembly in 1941 employing a huge prop that depicted the Great Speckled Bird. This captured the imagination of the church and the symbol became popular until the 1980s [See *Minutes of the Thirty-Sixth Annual Assembly*, 1941, 70-72, and note particularly the photograph on p.71. Homer wrote "The Great Speckled Bird" in

1941 [WHPC], a twenty-seven page manuscript, that magnified A. J. Tomlinson and his followers, and envisioned the ecumenical gathering of all Christians into the Church of God.

244"The Great Speckled Bird," 2-5.

245Elizabeth Schalappi, *Roy Acuff: The Smoky Mountain Boy*, 1980, 25-26; Dorothy Harstman, *Sing Your Heart Out Country Boy*, 1986, 46-47.

246*Catalog of Copyright Entries*, 1937, Vol. 23-Pt.1, P.8809; and see *Roy Acuff*, 25, and footnote on that page.

247*Catalog of Copyright Entries*, 1941, Vol. 27-Pt.3, CR. 48526.

248Apparently Homer did not know the history of the song, and gave credit to Sarah Dillon for its composition and melody ["The Great Speckled Bird," 1]. He took credit himself for its first copyright [Ibid] which is incorrect [see notes 243-247].

249In the late 1970s some of the ministers began to question the lyrics as being a proper interpretation of Jeremiah 12:9. But little stir was made until Joseph Bathe, the pastor of the Keith Street Church in Cleveland, challenged the lyrics and implications of the song in a sermon delivered on a Sunday morning in 1985. Thereafter, the popularity of the song waned and the motif faded.

250Quakers have been historically egalitarian and well-known for their anti-slavery position in the United States even in the eighteenth century. Tomlinson was reared in Westfield, Indiana with this magnanimous view of humanity; and his vision of the world and humanity was enlarged at Westfield's Union Academy in the mid-1880s. He was a northerner as well as a Quaker, and this added a larger vision for the church in its Appalachian setting, particularly in the late nineteenth and early twentieth centuries. But his dynamic baptism in the Spirit, increased his universal view of humanity and vision of God's church. While in the ecstasy of the Spirit on January 12, 1908, he claimed to have been carried in a vision to many continents and countries and to have spoken in at least ten different languages [**Conflict,** 234-236].

251The transcendence of Jim Crows laws, however, was a common ocurrence among Pentecostals in general. People of all races and nationalities found affinity in the "latter rain" of the outpoured Spirit. Frank Bartleman, the famous reporter of the Azusa Street revival, was fascinated by the indiscriminate blending of races and cultures among early Pentecostals, and proclaimed, "The color line has been washed away by the blood." But Tomlinson and his followers often crossed the line as a matter of principle. Note his annual addresses in 1935 [**Historical Annual Addresses**, Vol. 2, 249-251] and 1941 [Ibid, Vol.3, 208-210].

[252]*Minutes of the Thirty-Sixth Annual Assembly*, 1941, 30-31, 87-88.

[253]Women ministries were recognized in the church from the beginning. There is secondary source evidence that admits Spurling licensed Dorcas (Freeman) Bowers between 1892-1895 in the Christian Union congregation that he organized at Pine Ridge. Spurling implied this probability in his letter to Tomlinson on November 6, 1932 [WHPC]. Women participated in the discussions in the First Assembly [*General Assembly Minutes 1906-1914*, 15], and the role of deaconess was recognized in the Third Assembly [Ibid,49]. Nevertheless, women's roles were always considered subservient to men's in regard to the government and business of the church. "Here is where women are to keep silence: that is, they are to have no active part in the governmental affairs (1 Cor.14:34). . . . There were no women speaking in the council at Jerusalem . . ." [Conflict, 71].

[254]*Minutes of the Thirty-Sixth Annual Assembly*, 1941, 75-76.

[255]*Minutes of the Thirty-Fourth Annual Assembly*, 1939, 104.

[256]*Minutes of the Thirty-Eighth Annual Assembly*, 1943, 74-75.

[257]Tomlinson made this declaration in an address before the Cleveland Chamber of Commerce on April 16, 1935. It was made in part to help solicit funds to build a new Assembly tabernacle. He concluded his address in his usual cheerleading style: "In conclusion I shout, hurrah for our Cleveland, the capital of the world for the Church of God, and our big magnifical tabernacle that our Cleveland is going to help us to construct" [**Historical Annual Addresses,** Vol. 2], 237-238. Tomlinson made it clear to the Assembly delegates that he felt Cleveland was chosen by God to be the world headquarters for the Church of God [Ibid].

[258]Tomlinson had carefully planned his funeral after suffering a severe illness in 1937 from which he later recovered. But the script was followed upon his death in 1943 [Funeral Script, WHPC; and see **Upon This Rock,** Vol. 2, 874-875; Vol. 3, 15-65; Duggar, **Tomlinson,** 759-768] for details and photographs of the funeral.

[259]Tomlinson's annual address in 1943 presented a view of the church's future that was highly idealistic. He envisioned complete joy and victory for the church without persecution, and seemed to intimate a univeralism [**Historical Annual Addresses,** Vol.3], 246-247. This perception was all the more remarkable in view of the fact that the world was then embroiled in war, which the United States had entered on December 7, 1941. The exultation—"I see nothing but victories on top of victories for the Church of God"—was repeated in the the special called meeting of the overseers to select an interim General Overseer [October 7, 1943], and it had appeared also in the last issue of the *White Wing Messenger* [front page] before the overseer's historic meeting.

[260]Homer, **Diary,** Vol. 2, 98-112, and see photograph on inside cover.

[261]Ibid.

[262]A. J. Tomlinson mortgaged a piece of property in order to finance Homer's education at the University of Tennessee [1910-1912]. See "Opinion," *Church of God vs. A. J. Tomlinson,* 8.

[263]This inrepretation was given by Charles W. Batson ("Minutes of Special Overseer's Meeting," October 7, 1943, 15-16 [WHPC]), who had been appointed with Harper Hunter Jr. as state overseer of Maine [*Minutes of the Thirty-Eighth Annual Assembly,* 1943, 80-81]. An overriding concept that seemed to guide the conference, however, was that the General Overseer must be one who was "born in Zion." This was first suggested by C. H. Holley ["Minutes of Overseers," 7], then overseer of Cuba, referring to Psalms 87:5 and interpreted to mean that the new General Overseer would be one who had his natural birth after June 13, 1903, the day that A. J. Tomlinson was said to have "found the church." Holley later said that he did not "believe the [position] would leave the family" [p.8]. Thus, since Milton was born in 1906 and Homer in 1892, Holley implied Milton. Guy Marlow and a few thought Homer should have been selected [Marlow defected with Homer after 1943]. Some thought that Avery D. Evans, Tomlinson's son-in-law, should be selected, and thus Homer accused Evans later of forming a conspiracy for the office, assisted by his wife, Iris, L.A. Moxley, and S. O. Gillaspie [Homer, **Diary,** Vol. 2, 100-109].

[264]Homer returned to New York and soon denounced the Overseer's decision, and began to circulate his conspiracy theory [Homer, **Diary,** 100-109; and see note 263]. Meanwhile testimonies were received in Cleveland from Iris M. Evans and Grady R. Kent that contradicted Homer's interpretation of his father's comment in the April 18, 1943 issue of the *White Wing Messenger*. Several brethren [including Milton] from Cleveland traveled to New York and failed in an attempt to reconcile Homer. Following this effort Milton revoked Homer's license, and relieved him of his positions in the church, which included State Overseer of New York and Foreign Language Secretary. Milton placed a notice in the *White Wing Messenger* [November 27, 1943] stating the same, which occasioned more resentment in Homer. Thereafter Homer summoned a conference of his followers in New York scheduled for December 7-9, 1943, and was "confirmed in his position" with "mighty anointings" [Ibid, 110]. But see Davidson [**Upon This Rock**, 88-95] for a different interpretation of these events. Davidson's views are particularly noteworthy since he was appointed as overseer of New York upon Homer's defection, and because he was personally acquainted with Homer for a number of years. He also attended Homer's conference in New York, December 7-9, 1943 [Ibid].

[265]Homer Tomlinson was a gifted writer and journalist. He had a knack for advertisement and publicity; he knew how to draw attention to a person or issue. He had served the church for years in promotions of all kinds, exciting public interest in the church and its programs. But he had an eccentric side, which became more acute as he grew older. Upon his father's death he began to have delusions about his calling and purpose. He reflected in his later years that this peculiar calling came to him at fifteen years of age ["Called to be President of the United States," *The Church of God Sunday School Quarterly*, July-September, 1957, 2]. These delusions became more bazaar after his defection in 1943, which he was able to act upon since he was no longer under the government and discipline of the church. Three times he attempted to become the President of the United States campaigning on the "Theocratic Party" ticket. The platform for his campaigns included uniting church and state in a "kingdom of righteousness." His

overrealized eschatology occasioned him to declare himself "King of All Nations of Men" on September 4, 1954 promising world peace. This began in Greeneville, Tennessee and included a coronation service, which he replicated in over one hundred countries around the world [see William Whitworth, "Profiles: On the Tide of the Times," *The New Yorker*, September 24, 1966, 67,70]. His campaign gimmicks got him engagements to speak in prominent universities, including Yale, Harvard, and Princeton, where he proposed abolishing taxes in favor of tithing; declaring prohibitions on divorce, gambling, the use of drugs, liquor, and tobacco; and establishing racial equality. He envisioned moving the United Nations to Jerusalem, replacing ambassadors with preachers, and establishing himself upon the restored Throne of David [Ibid, 77-78, 103-105]. In 1954 he claimed that a small country named Druze located between Amman in Jordan and Damascus in Syria deeded its land to The Church of God, which Homer named *Ecclesia* [Latin spelling of the Greek word translated "church"], and thus he became King Homer I of Ecclesia [Ibid, 81- 82]. His campaign in 1960 at Princeton University nearly set off a riot, after he excited the passions of students by predicting that he would be elected "by a miracle" [Ibid]. In 1964 Homer failed for the third time in his bid for the presidency of the United States, campaigning from his porch in Queens, New York. Thereafter he served as campaign manager for Bishop Bill Rogers, the overseer of his churches in Missouri. Homer died on December 4, 1968.

[266]This may be seen even in the overseers' meeting on October 7, 1943. There was a prevailing sentiment that A. J. Tomlinson was the antitype of Moses, and that he had envisioned the complete fulfillment of the church's mission in this world. Milton A. Tomlinson was thus selected because he embodied the spirit of his father; and as the antitype of Joshua, he was simply to complete the prophetic journey begun in "Moses" [i.e., his father]. This view was set forth in 1964 by Lillie Duggar: "Without A. J. Tomlinson there would be no vision of the church and the great things it is destined to accomplish. The vision was revealed to him and he has passed it on to others...his vision is all we know. And the Church of God has not yet reached the end of his vision...And it is believed by some

that his vision reached even to the end when the work will all be done and every prophecy fulfilled, and by reading some of his writings concerning the future there can be little doubt, if any, that this view is correct" [**A. J. Tomlinson,** 228; and see also Introduction]. This opinion prevailed for the next three decades in the church.

267This may be seen in his first two annual addresses [1944-1945]. See also Davidson, **Fields of the Wood,** 1948, 43-78. L. S. Rhodes was appointed manager of Fields of the Wood in 1944, but Kent was clearly the overwhelming influence. His charima, inspiration, and vision, excited the passions of the church, and began an era in the church which lived in the expectation of "fulfilling prophecy." The new General Overseer himself, in large measure, rode the wave of Kent's prophetic visions and apocalyptic expectations.

268Moxley was Bible Training Camp's first superintendent, appointed by Tomlinson in 1945 [*Minutes of Forty-First Annual Assembly*, 1946, 30-31]; but A. D. Evans had been a zealous advocate for the camp since 1941. The camp became more institutionalized and authoritative after 1948 under the leadership of J. B. Wright.

269His comments in his annual address in 1913 were typical: "As we enter the business of this Assembly we should bear in mind that the eyes of thousands are and will be upon us...The Assembly of the Church of God has reached a plans of stupendous immensity. It is no more the tender plant unknown and unknowing as at the time of its birth on the twenty-sixth and twenty-seventh days of January, seven years ago . . . At the time of its birth it was not known whether it would live or die; but time and evidences prove that it was destined to live and make its mark in the world . . . It is not too much to say that every state in the Union will hear the voice of this Assembly. Canada, South America, Europe, Asia, Africa and many of the islands of the sea will bear the sound that goes from the platform of this auditorium . . . Knowing the far-reaching influence of this . . . that we are making history should surely be an incentive for us to do our best" [**Historical Annual Addresses**, Vol. 1, 20-21]. A little later in the same address, he noted, "The Church of God is the greatest, wisest and most glorious government that has ever been inaugurated on this earth. To be called upon, as is this honorable body and sacred Assembly, to search out and apply the laws of the greatest, wisest and most glorious government that has ever made its appearance on this earth, should surely be considered the highest honor conferred upon man...No people on earth have been called upon to occupy such an exalted position" [Ibid, 24]. A little further, he said, "A national government cannot exist without statesmen. What would the United States government have ever accomplished without Washington, Webster, Jefferson, Lincoln, Garfield, McKinley and many others of their equal? . . . much more must the Church of God have men versed in the art of government . . . At this Assembly we should earnestly seek to reinstate and re-establish the government under whose banner the brave apostles and their contemporaries fought, bled and died to sustain . . ." [Ibid, 24-25].

[270]It should be remembered that Tomlinson was extremely zealous for national politics before his conversion [**Answering the Call**, 4], and though after his conversion his "interest in politics vanished" and he never voted again [Ibid, 9-10], yet he had been more deeply affected evidently than he knew. In many ways he simply transposed the developing government of the Church of God over American political ideas and traditions [See Phillips, "The Church of God: A Portrait of America," 68-84; and "Transformed Tomlinson," 14n39]. But Tomlinson was encouraged and assisted in this direction by Lee Llewellyn, and others. See Lee's address, "Confirmation of Actions of Past Assemblies" [*General Assembly Minutes 1906-1914*, 180-189]. This trend became especially noticeable when the infamous constitution was drafted in 1921, which began with the words, "We the people in order to form a more perfect union. . . ." There are also indications that the developing constitutional system was patterned after the bi-cameral system of America's congress. The Twelve and Seventy were designed to function apparently similar to the Senate and house.

[271]"If we can receive it, even our pattern at Jerusalem, where the honorable and illustrious James was moderator and his contemporary Peter was the principle [*sic*] speaker, does not surpass this Assembly in importance and honor" [**Historical Annual Addresses,** Vol.1, 24].

[272]The praise and honor that Tomlinson gave to James, the Lord's brother, in his annual addresses between 1913-

1917 were strange indeed. He described him in regal terms and symbols, imagining that "he sat upon his imperial and mediatorial throne" [**Historical Annual Addresses,** Vol.1, 40]. This was said in order to establish his own position in the church as General Overseer, which he maintained was the antitype of Moses' in Israel [Ibid; and see "Transformed Tomlinson," 13-25].

[273]A. D. Evans, **The Business End of the Church of God** (Cleveland,TN: WWPH, 1933), 45.

[274]Ibid.

[275]The initial injunction filed on February 26, 1924 would prove to be a long and expensive litigation that would not be settled finally until May 1, 1952. Bradley Chancery Court ruled in favor of the Llewellyn-Lee faction [Opinion and Decree of Chancellor, *Church of God, et als., vs. A. J. Tomlinson, et als.* Number 1891, WHPC], and the church was forbidden to use the name, Church of God; but on March 12, 1924 at Jasper, TN, Chancellor T. L. Stewart modified the injunction [on account of a demurrer having been filed] so that the church could continue to operate with restraints under the title "Church of God, over which A. J. Tomlinson is General Overseer" [George E.Westerburg and Arthur Traynor, counsel for defendants, "A Concise Statement of the Church Litigation Now Pending in the Chancery Court at Cleveland, Tennessee," WHPC]. The conditions were ackward, however, as the ministers were required always to explain the injunction to candidates for membership and ministry, and, moreover, they could not claim to be the true church to the exclusion of the com-plainants, nor could they publish literature or the church's paper under the name, Church of God, nor deny that Llewellyn, Lee, and Ellis, were officials of the church and defenders of its doctrines [Ibid]. Meanwhile the origi-nal bill was appealed by the church, and on July 3, 1925, the Tennessee Court of Appeals ruled completely in favor of Tomlinson and his followers, repealing the decree of the Chancellor ["Opinion," *Church of God vs. A. J. Tomlinson, et al;* WHPC]. This was a great victory but shortlived. The Lewellyn-Lee faction appealed to the State Supreme Court and, on July 15, 1927, the court ruled entirely in favor of the complainants, reversing the decision of the Appellate Court and affirming the decree of the chancellor ["Opinion" of the Supreme Court, Bradley Equity, *The Church of God*

vs. A. J. Tomlinson et al., WHPC]. A petition was prepared for a new hearing but denied. The decision was final. After being arrested with Lawson and Evans for contempt of court [for using the name, Church of God], Tomlinson appealed again to the court for some mitigation. On April 8, 1929 the Church's three officials appeared before Honorable T. L. Stewart again, with an attorney provided *gratis* by the Chamber of Commerce, and the court ruled in favor of the church's suggestion that the name, Tomlinson, be added as a prefix to Church of God. Thus the church became the Tomlinson Church of God [*Church of God vs. A. J. Tomlinson, et al.* Chancery Court Of Bradley County, Tenn.]. As soon as news of this reached the field, an array of protest was raised against the Tomlinson prefix. Tomlinson attempted to excuse the prefix by explaining that the name was not Tomlinson's Church of God but Tomlinson Church of God; but this met with complete dissatisfaction and a delegation of ministers from Virginia made a trip to Cleveland on May 7, 1929 to counsel with the General Overseer about the matter. This resulted in another petition being filed on May 8th. During the Assembly on September 14, 1929, a resolution was adopted to distinguish the church by the designation, "Church of God, A. J. Tomlinson General Overseer" ["Preamble and Resolution," Questions and Subjects Committee Report]. This was a lengthy resolution that expressed the Assembly's deep affection and religious consciousness ". . . that the name CHURCH OF GOD is a sacred name to us because it is a Bible name, and to be deprived of the free use of it would so stifle and afflict our consciences that discouragement and despair would constantly grind us down so we would scarcely have a heart and courage to maintain our orphanage work, keep our missionaries and workers on the fields, and maintain the institution in a general way" [*Minutes of the Twenty-Fourth Annual Assembly*, 1929]. Meanwhile the church's officials were again arrested and fined [brought before the court on May 25 and again on May 31]. The court denied the petition filed on May 8th [the legal name of the church remained Tomlinson Church of God], but allowed some relief to use the name Church of God over which A. J. Tomlinson is General Overseer [Tomlinson, **Diary,** January 1, 1930]. The opposing faction insisted on a strict remained Tomlinson Church of God], but allowed some relief to use the name Church of God over which A. J. Tomlinson is General Overseer [Tomlinson, **Diary,** January 1, 1930]. The opposing faction insisted on a strict compliance to the court rulings through the years [Ibid, April 11, 1932], which Tomlinson seemed to take lightly [he was punished for contempt in 1932 and 1936; Virgil Carmichael, "Background of Litigation," 1]. This kept the antagonism alive through the next generation.

[276]Ibid.

[277]Ibid.

[278]*H. L. Chesser Et Al vs. M. A. Tomlinson Et Al.*, May 1, 1952; and see note 275.

[279]*Church of God (H. L. Chesser, Zeno C. Tharp et al) vs. THE TOMLINSON CHURCH OF GOD, or CHURCH OF GOD OF PROPHECY (M. A. Tomlinson, J. R. Kinser et al*; Cause No. 1891; Chancery Court).

This was more than relief for the name, for the church was charged with contempt again in the early part of 1952 which reached the Supreme Court. Thus the church stood convicted before the highest court in Tennessee [Carmichael, "Background of Litigation," 2]. After acceptance of the terms of Judge Woodlee, and a compliance was made within ninety days [to change deeds, signs, stationary, etc. into the name Church of God of Prophecy] the contempt petition was dropped [Ibid, 2-3].

[280]Note Tomlinson's annual address in 1941 [**Historical Annual Addresses**, Vol. 3, 193-194] and Milton's annual address in 1953 [*Forty-Seventh Annual Assembly*, 1953, 28-30].

[281]This story was carried in the *Cleveland Banner* and in *Newsweek* [November 9, 1953, 42:92, 92].

[282]See *Newsweek* [November 9, 1953, 92].

[283]Ibid.

[284]Kent was licensed June 22, 1932; appointed overseer of Vermont in 1935, Minnesota in 1936, and Nebraska for two years from 1937-1938 ["Kent File," WHPC; C. T. Davidson, ed., **Memoirs Of Our Ministry** [Cleveland, TN: WWPH, 1949].

[285]Ibid.

286The incident gained greater notoreity in the church after Kent published **Flogged by KU KLUX KLAN** [WWHP, 1942], a forty-five page booklet that dramatized the incident with photographs, including the trial.

287**Flogged** 5-19.

288Ibid, 30-31; **Memoirs,** "Grady R. Kent."

289Davidson, **Fields of the Wood**, 19-20; Phillips, conversations with E. H. Griffith, 1983-1987. Griffith was serving on the general staff during the these events, and was a member with Tomlinson of the Cleveland church where Kent pastored. He was thus well-informed and a primary eyewitness.

290See Tomlinson's 1941 annual address [**Historical Annual Addresses**, Vol.3, 194-199].

291*Minutes of Thirty-Eighth Annual Assembly*, 1943, 81; Kent was A. J. Tomlinson's last official appointment as General Overseer.

292This project grew out of the "Arise, Shine" enthusiasm beginning in 1939. The planes were thus depicted as "Flying Arise Shine markers" carry the "voice of prophecy," Grady R. Kent, "The Message By Wings," tract [Cleveland,TN: WWHP, 1953]; "Wings of Prophecy Evangelistic Association," *Souvenir Program* [WHPC]; *Wings of Prophecy Monthly Bulletin* [Cleveland, TN: WWHP, December 1, 1952, 1:2, 2; Grady R. Kent, "Biblical Wonder of the Twentieth Century," [Cleveland, TN: WWHP, n.d.].

293Like Homer Tomlinson, Kent had a knack for publicity and drew considerable public attention by his air shows. Some of his favorite passages used to support the "Wings of Prophecy" were Isaiah 60:1; Ecclesiastes 10:20; Ezekiel 10:1-9; Revelation 14:6-7. Many on-lookers, however, criticized the whole airplane program as "a flying circus." Some of the ministers in the church thought the money used for the White Angel Fleet could be better spent on education [but inside critics maintained a low profile due to the overwhelming popularity of the program].

294Taped message, 1952, cassette [WHPC].

295The subject had been argued in the manner of the Roman Church on the issue of the authority of the pope in regard to ecumenical councils. A. J. Tomlinson had said on occasion that he was "more or less" subject to the Assembly, but when tested in 1921-1923 he clearly came down on the side of the ultimate authority of the General Overseer. Those that followed him in the revolution after 1923 were doubtlessly under the same impression. This was the prevailing opinion until Tomlinson died in 1943, and for that same reason it was not an issue while he lived, that is, 1923 seemed to have settled it. The weaker image of Milton probably occasioned the issue to surface again. In any case, the issue of the final word in the church was addressed and settled in the Assembly in 1948: "BE IT RESOLVED . . . the General Assembly is the highest authority in the Church" ["Questions and Subjects Committee Report," *Minutes of the Forty-Third Annual Assembly*, 1948, 124-125]. Milton conceded to this resolution, which displeased Kent. Thereafter Kent maintained that the church was a democracy rather than a theocracy under the resolution. Wright's strong conviction about the matter was soon reflected in Bible Training Camp's curriculum [*Lessons in Bible Training*, Vol.2, 52, under "Church Business"].

[296]Grady R. Kent, "The Battle Rages: Declaration," *The Vision Speaks* [Cleveland, TN: 258 Broad Street] April, 1957,1:1, 1-3. This was the first issue of Kent's new paper, which provided him space to denounce the Church of God of Prophecy, to explain his dissenting views, and to promote the idea that he was continuing the same vision and revelation of A. J. Tomlinson "in its complete form" [Ibid]. This was a recurring theme in the following months and years in order to gain converts and proselytize Church of God of Prophecy members. [See also Grady R. Kent, "Historical Words," *The Vision Speaks*, May 1957, 4; "Without the Bible We Would Not Know," December, 1958, 3; et al].

[297]Questions and Subjects Committee Report, Section 4: "Question. Does the church endorse attempts by its ministers to identify themselves or other ministers as the two witnesses mentioned in Revelation 11? Does it approve of anyone indicating that he is John the Revelator? Answer. No" [*Minutes of the Fifty-First Annual Assembly*, 1956, 110-111]. Clearly this was directed at Kent and his followers.

[298]Kent's resignation was published in *The Vision Speaks* [January 1958, 4], in which he explained his reasons.

[299]Ibid; and see June 1960 issue, 3. Kent's reform movement was dated with his resignation on February 13, 1957. See "Chief Bishop Declares Vacancies," *The Vision Speaks* [November 1957, 2]. The general sentiment of Kent's followers was "The only amendments or repentance that will count NOW is to follow Bro. Grady R. Kent who has saved The Church of God again!" ["Why Be Deceived? These Truths Are Self Evident!", *The Vision Speaks*, August 1957, 4].

[300]Like Homer Tomlinson, Kent's behavior became more bazaar after he left the church. Without the government and discipline of his peers, his imagination was allowed to soar among his followers. Some of his followers were identified as "last days" apostles, ordained and endowed with special wisdom and knowledge into the mysteries of God's prophetic plan. The group took on a cultish character, exclusive, and with peculiar revelations. Kent and the "apostles" grew beards and carried staffs. The apostles were given new names identified with the precious stones in the foundation of new Jerusalem [Revelation 21: 19-20] and actually became designated by the name of the gems. Marion Hall became Marion Emerald Hall; and thus David Sardonyx Williams, Earl Jacinth Steward, R. L. Amethyst Simmons, and so on. [See, e.g., Apostle Earl Jacinth, "Voice of the Bird of the Air," *The Vision Speaks*, 4]. Added to these Twelve, "Seven Men of Wonder" were chosen to direct the seven auxiliaries of the church [*The Vision Speaks*, August, 1960, 4]. On one occasion Kent shaved his head and trimmed his beard, put his hair into a black parachute and dropped it while flying over Fields of the Wood. This was staged while the Church of God of Prophecy was celebrating the "Arise Shine" of the Church on June 13, 1960. The headlines of the next issue of *The Vision Speaks* declared, "St. John II Pronounces Cutting Off Of Thousands" [July 1960]. The claim of the article was that the event fulfilled a "major prophecy," namely Ezekiel 8:1-3. This was Kent's final call to the Church of God of Prophecy for repentance for what they had done to him and for refusing to submit to his divine call as St. John II or John the Revelator [Ibid, 1-3]. The headlines of the pre-

vious issue of *The Vision Speaks* declared, "Victorious Reformation Ends," with an article entitled, "Chief Bishop Declares Desolation of Old House" [June 1960, 1].

[301]Milton highly regarded his father's appointments, which allowed a powerful body of overseers to develop during his tenure. One esteemed overseer was often quoted as saying, "This is an overseer's church." This development was resented by the next generation , which became problematic by the 1980s.

[302]Questions and Subjects Committee Report, *Minutes of the Forty-Seventh Annual Assembly*, 1952. This report was supported by the same committee in *Fifty-First Annual Assembly*, 1957, Section 7, 136.

[303]There was, of course, a vivid lingering of the memory of A. J. Tomlinson in the hearts and minds of the older generation. Among many of these the former General Overseer was still venerated and remembered with a sense of deep reverence. Even as late as 1967, the assistant editor of the *White Wing Messenger* wrote an article entitled, "Why Quote A. J. Tomlinson?", in which he said, "WE QUOTE A. J. TOMLINSON BECAUSE he spoke and wrote with an authoritative positiveness unequalled by anything short of the very Word of God. In fact, his words are so compatible with truth, so confirmed by the inspired writings of the Bible authors, that one can scarcely question them without a feeling of futility. (I am referring to those who have read after him, laying his writings alongside the Sacred Writ.) Only men with whom God has dealt can write with such unfaltering affirmation . . ."[*White Wing Messenger*, September 9, 1967, 15].

[304]"The Passing of the Gavel," *White Wing Messenger*, May 26, 1990, 4.

[305]*Call Council*, 3.

[306]**Historical Annual Addresses,** Vol.1, 223-224.

[307]The objective for creating Bible Training Camp was clearly stated in the Questions and Subjects Committee Report in 1939: ". . . our members must be informed in order that they may effectively and efficiently cooperate with the Assembly, with the Overseers of territories, with the District Overseers, with the Pastors and with the Auxiliary Leaders. Therefore, we wish to recommend that this

Assembly take into consideration and adopt the following measures for the promotion of the Church of God and the maintaining of the high standard of doctrine for which the church so strongly stands" [*Minutes of the Thirty-Forth Annual Assembly*, 1939, 103]. Later under Wright's superintendency an extreme authoritarian posture was given to Bible Training Camp. Students were drilled in "established doctrine and practices." Wright noted in his Assembly report in 1950, "More and more I feel that the Training Camp is providing . . . invaluable service toward producing and preserving the unity of doctrine and praactice among our ministry and laity." [*Minutes of the Forty-Fifth Annual Assembly*, 1950, 67].

[308]In general it had been felt that Tomlinson Memorial School was not sufficiently meeting the educational needs of the church; but insufficient finances were also a major factor in closing the school in 1963. The outcome was finally determined by the school Board. [See Questions and Subjects Committee Report, *Minutes of the Fifty-Eighth Annual Assembly*, 1963, and General Overseer's annual address, *Minutes of the Fifty-Ninth Annual Assembly*, 1964, 38-41].

[309]In its first year Tomlinson College operated at Madisonville, Tennessee. The next year the college was moved to Cleveland "because of certain advantages" and occupied the building formerly used by Tomlinson Memorial School. Since this was conveniently located on the orphanage property, the Questions and Subjects Committee recommended that Tomlinson Home for Children deed to Tomlinson College a portion of the land. Later the orphanage in Cleveland was discontinued which left the entire property to the college [See Questions and Subjects Committee report, *Minutes of the Sixty-Second Annual Assembly*, 1967, Section 4].

[310]See notes 340-341.

[311]Moore had risen to prominence after his appointment in 1951 to the position of General Secretary for youth ministries ["Victory Leaders"]. Thereafter he served under general appointment in a number of capacities, including Radio Minister. He was also one of the best known ministers outside the church. He had been appointed President

of Tomlinson College at the Assembly in 1976. His tragic suicide sent shock waves and disillusionment through the church [See his tribute in *White Wing Messenger*, November 6, 1976, 4].

[312]See Questions and Subjects Committee Report, *Minutes of the Sixty-Second Annual Assembly*, 1967, Section 2, 382; and Ways and means Committee Report, *Minutes of the Sixty-Third Annual*, 1968, Section 4.

[313]See General Overseer's annual address, *Minutes of the Sixty- Sixth Annual Assembly*, 1971, 54-55; Questions and Subjects Committee Report, Ibid, Sections 3-4; and General Overseer's annual address, "Our Headquarters Complex," *Minutes of the Sixty- Ninth Annual Assembly*, 1974, 49.

[314]Ibid, 56-58; and see *White Wing Messenger*, September 2, 1972, front cover, and September 16, 1972, 1-9.

[315]See General Overseer's annual address, "Our Headquarters Complex," *Minutes of the Sixty-Ninth Annual Assembly*, 1974, 49.

[316]He made this admission to the writer during a conversation in the Summer of 1983, while we were discussing plans for the up-coming Assembly program [the writer was, at that time, General Secretary of the Church of Prophecy Marker Association, Fields of the Wood Manager, and Chief Usher of the General Assembly]. At that same time he expressed some concern with a traditional view that his time could expire by divine intervention after fulfilling his forty years in office [which would have concluded October 7, 1983].

[317]The selection of Murray was not without strong resistance. Several sternly opposed his nomination, and insisted that the chair recognize other nominations. A. J. Coalter and J. E. Brisson were then nominated. After hours of questioning the nominees and further debate, the body of presbyters were unable to agree on a single nominee. Brice Thompson had been selected to chair the meeting, and called the presbyters to prayer to seek the face of the Lord for guidance and revelation. The body was in general moved by the presence of the Spirit during prayer, but remained divided in opinion. Murray had received a majority of the "votes," but procedure called for unanimity. Finally, on May 2nd after further prayer and debate, those

who remained strongly opposed to Murray conceded to his selection as interim General Overseer.[*Minutes of Special Called Presbytery Meeting, April 30-May 2, 1990*, 179-194]. Some submitted anticipating the selection to be overturned in the General Assembly [see notes 318, 329]. Their hopes were defeated. Murray was selected without a dissenting voice, amidst overwhelming rejoicing with tongues and interpretations approving his selection [*Minutes of the Eighty-Fifth Annual Assembly*, 1990, 13-16].

[318]Some came to the Assembly fully intending to overturn Murray's selection, but were so overwhelmed by the general consent and favor of the delegates, and the apparent approval of God himself, that they offered no dissenting voice [Ibid]. The writer was at the platform during this selection process, and stood beside two gentlemen waiting to oppose Murray's selection [these two men among others had made their opinions known]. After a message in tongues and interpretation approved of Murray, followed by much rejoicing among delegates, Murray noticed the brethren and asked one of them if he would like to speak. The gentleman paused, then walked away from the platform; the other brother followed him. No one was left at the platform to resist his selection. Robert Pruitt, who later denied the legitmacy of Murray's selection, ironically made Murray's selection a matter of official record by signing the Assembly minutes in his capacity as chief clerk.

[319]See notes 317-319, 329.

[320]See Questions and Subjects Committee Report, Section 1, *Minutes of the Eighty-Fifth Annual Assembly*, 1990, 43.

[321]"In Memoriam: Milton Ambrose Tomlinson," *White Wing Messenger*, Special Edition, May 20, 1995. This entire edition was dedicated to the memory of Tomlinson.

[322]A. J. Tomlinson was selected as General Moderator in January 1909. The title was changed to General Overseer in 1910. [See notes 75-78, 135-136]. His tenure was perpetuated among his followers after the disruption in 1923 until his death in 1943. Thus Milton's resignation on April 30, 1990 made eighty years and seven months that he and his father had held the office.

[323]A. J. Tomlinson's birth [1865] to Milton's death [1995] spanned 130 years.

[324]The office of General Overseer had been developed as the antitype of Moses' position in "the church in the wilderness" [See A. J. Tomlinson's annual addresses 1913-1914; Davidson, **Fields of the Wood,** 1-20]. Tomlinson's death in 1943 deepened the impression of the antitype, for his forty years of leadership in the church [1903-1943] seemed to coincide with Moses' forty years in Israel. Moreover, since other biblical leaders served for forty years [Solomon and Elijah, e.g.] the tenure seemed to be a divine appointment for the sacred office. This interpretation was quite common during Milton's tenure, and deeply impressed him.

[325]"You all can do that after I leave," or some variable of that expression, was not an uncommon response by Milton during his last ten years in office. He did not necessarily disagree with some of the new proposals and issues, but seemed to dread the "hassel"—the controversies, heated debates, and so on—that were more or less part of the process toward settlement. And quite often controversial issues could not be settled in peace and harmony, which discouraged weaker members and created schismatic factions. Thus it seemed wisdom to him to avoid issues and problems that disturbed the peace of the church. On the other hand, many ministers felt frustrated by the static process, and complained about a system "frozen in time," "outdated," and "irrelevant."

[326]One minister remarked that this "table" was not large enough to hold all the unsettled issues.

[327]Issues related to doctrine, polity, government, organization, and finance, were all needing addressed.

[328]The complaints against Murray were never in regard to his personal integrity, but against his points of view concerning certain doctrines and traditions in the church. He represented change, which some interpreted to be "liberal" and "compromising." One minister remarked that "he is weak as water," though the vast majority of the church would have considered this sentiment completely unjustified. The distrust of Murray's doctrinal views was clearly expressed during the presbytery meeting on May 1,1990 [see comments by various prebyters, *Overseer's Meeting*, 101-119].

[329]The complaints began during the presbytery meeting when Murray was nominated to be the interim General Overseer. After his selection was approved against a small group of dissenters who finally submitted, many false reports went out that distorted the facts of the meeting. It was reported that M. A. Tomlinson was forced to step down from office by "adamant and belligerent" men who "were determined to have their way" [e.g., see Letter from Donald R. Estep to Billy Murray, published in *The Evening Light*, August 1993, 4-6]. Nevertheless the minutes and audio cassettes of the meeting clearly show that the men referred to merely persisted (respectfully) that the rulings of the Assembly be upheld, for the Assembly had decreed the order and course of action to be taken in the event that the General Overseer should become disabled [Questions and Subjects Committee Report, *Minutes of the Eighty- Forth Annual Assembly* 1989, 131]. The procedure made it clear that the office had to be vacated before the presbytery could meet and select the new General Overseer. Tomlinson had admitted that "I'm physically not able to continue...because of my disability" [*Overseers' Meeting*, 15]; but he was reluctant to comply with the Assembly ruling in order that he might reserve the right to approve or reject the person selected by the overseers [See Hugh Edwards remarks, Ibid, 10-11]; and thus the meeting was locked in debate until Tomlinson complied with the ruling. Finally he acknowledged, "Well, it looks like . . . what I'm going to have to do is just declare the office vacant because of my disability and let you all go ahead with your business" [Ibid]. Upon this there was an applause of approval [Ibid]. After Murray had been selected, "The Concerned Group" maintained that he had been selected by a "split vote" of 48 to 33, and that it was "the first time for the church to act outside unanimity" ["The Concerned For Bible Doctrine," *The Evening Light*, March 1993, 3]. This was another false report. It is true that a vote was taken that showed 48 for Murray and 33 for A. J. Coalter. Upon that, however, Hector Ortiz, then State Overseer of Ohio, said that he had voted for Coalter but that God had confirmed to him that Murray "is the man"

[*Overseers' Meeting*, 177]. This brought an "outburst of shouting and praise" [Ibid] and thereupon several felt that God had manifested His approval of Murray. Another vote was not taken at that time, but thereafter only a small number remained against Murray. Some of these were outspoken but said they would submit [Ibid, 179-195]. The lone hold-out who felt that he could not submit seemed to be the State Overseer of Iowa, Russel Sullivan [Ibid, 190]. Several gathered around to pray with him until he was able to submit [Ibid, 191; the writer was one of those who prayed with him]. Thereupon, a spirit of praise came into the meeting and the room was filled with singing and worship [Ibid, 197-198]. Murray and Coalter were then brought into the meeting in the midst of praise. The Moderator, Brice Thompson, then addressed Murray and said, "Brother Murray, you've been selected, as you can see, unanimously, by this body to be the next General Overseer..." [Ibid, 198]. Upon this there was more praising [Ibid, 199]. Murray then spoke briefly and concluded the meeting [Ibid, 201]. These are the facts that are recorded and left as minutes of the meeting. The written minutes are perfectly consistent with the audio cassettes of the meeting. [See also notes 317-318].

330The General Overseer requested that Chairman Benny Jenkins call an emergency meeting of the Tomlinson College Board of Trustees on May 23, 1992. While in session, the General Overseer explained the financial crisis that the General church was facing. He indicated that the General Treasury could not supply the financial supplement needed to operate Tomlinson College. Several options were debated, but no alternative seemed adequate to keep the college afloat. Thus, the Trustees acted according to a memorandum from the Administrative Committee dated May 20, 1992, and suspended classes effective with the Fall semester 1992 [Report of the Tomlinson College Board of Trustees, *Minutes of the Eighty-Seventh Annual Assembly*, 1992, 153-155].

331An "Urgent Update" announcing the closing of the college was inserted in the next issue of the *White Wing Messenger*, June 6, 1992, 31. The issue coincidently featured a special section magnifying Tomlinson College and its future [already at press when the decision was made to close the college], which made the announcement satirical.

[332]In a special video tape prepared for pastors and overseers, Murray attempted to explain the circumstances surrounding the closing of the college and the financial crisis facing the International Offices. This was also published in the *White Wing Messenger* ["A Heartfelt Address," June 20, 1992, 3-5].

[333]Raymond Pruitt, a senior bishop with a good record of ministry and personal integrity, had for a long time disagreed with the church's traditional view on jewelry. But he did not make it an issue until the late 1980s. In 1987, while serving as State Overseer of Indiana, he wrote a paper entitled "The Jewelry Issue" and requested a few ministers to critique it. He then enlarged and edited the paper on September 14, 1988 with a new title—"The Adornment Issue." The paper received wide circulation and began to be debated by ministers and laymen on the field. Traditionalists raised a great protest against the paper and its author. Scores of complaints by letter and in person came to the General Overseer's office. Pruitt had been labeled "a liberal" which found a sympathetic ear in Tomlinson. And since the General Overseer controlled the Assembly agenda, he vowed that the issue would not come before the Assembly during his tenure, and rather insisted that ministers and members teach and practice the church's traditional "basic Bible beliefs" [See, e.g., his 1988 annual address, *Minutes of the Eighty-Third Annual Assembly*, 1988, 78-80]. Several ministers left the church in the following months and years, citing the adornment issue as their major frustration. But others who disagreed with the "prominent teaching" decided to wait out Tomlinson's tenure, anticipating progress and change with the next General Overseer. Meanwhile, the issue became passionately debated, with opponets clashing as often over personality differences as the issue itself. Ron Brisson, a young pastor in North Carolina, countered Pruitt's paper in 1989 with a book published by the church, entitled, **The Truth About Outward Adornment.** His book was endorsed by some of the church's leading traditionalists. Brisson later recanted, but for the moment his work

encouraged the cause of the traditionalists. At least two other papers were circulated to counter interpretations that favored changing or modifying the church's teaching "against wearing gold for ornament." But by 1990 there was "a flood rising behind the dam" that desired modification of the church's traditional stand.

[334]After the issue was studied further, the Committee presented a report that distinguished between wearing jewelry for occultic and idolatrous reasons, and as a harmless decoration [Questions and Subjects Committee Report, Section 3, *Minutes of the Eighty-Eighth Assembly*, 1994, 59-63]. The former was denounced, the latter left to the individual's conscience with some cautions [Ibid].

[335]Many traditionalists were not against allowing the wedding band *per se*, but anticipated that it would open the flood gate to members wearing jewelry in any form and for any reason. Still others feared that a change regarding the jewelry issue would lead to changes in other prominent doctrines, particularly the church's strict teaching against divorce and remarriage. [This sentiment was expressed to the writer by several leaders of the "Concerned For Bible Doctrine" group, e.g., George Sadler].

[336] See Questions and Subjects Committee Report, Section 1 Part F, *Eighty-Sixth Annual Assembly*, 1991, 83, 92, 109. Perhaps more important than the issue itself was the manner in which the Committee's report was passed. Never had an issue been passed in the Assembly with such a substantial number resisting it. Some, in fact, did not submit. The General Overseer simply declared the report approved according to what he judged to be an "overwhelming consensus" in favor of it [Ibid, 91]. This became a major complaint of "The Concerned Group" and gave occasion for an increase in their number. Even some who had no sympathy with this group were alarmed by the new way of doing business.

[337]The Concerned Group began to develop when several ministers and members in the church realized their common complaints, and their common desire to perpetuate the church's "twenty-nine prominent teachings," which had come to be viewed by them as a more or less infallible body

of doctrine [See Donald Estep's comments, *Overseers' Meeting*, 180; and messages and articles replete in *The Evening Light*, November 1992-October 1993]. The sentiment that "new light will not change old light" was a common expression among The Concerned Group, which more or less locked them into a creedal position on traditional statements of faith and practice. Equally important, however, was their desire to maintain traditional views of the nature and operation of "theocratic government," and the claim that the Church of God of Prophecy was God's only true church. The leaders of the group complained that "theocratic principles" had been transgressed in the selection of Murray during the presbytery meeting in May 1990 [See note 329; and "The Concerned For Bible Doctrine," *The Evening Light*, March 1993, 3]. As the group began to take form [against the counsel of the church's ruling elders] they adopted the name, "Concerned For Bible Doctrine," and began a publication in November 1992 called *The Evening Light*. Acting in large on suspicion and distrust (see, e.g.,Stephen E. Smith, "Being The Church Of God." *The Evening Light*, April 1993, 4) and against the counsel of their ruling elders, twenty-one representatives from this group met in Cleveland on August 20, 1992 and agreed together to turn their complaints against the new administration of the church into a legal case before the world. They retained an attorney in Chattanooga and began a prosecution against their brethren. While the lawsuit did not meet with approval of some who later joined the group, nevertheless they proceeded together in rebellion against the established government of the church. The August meeting in Cleveland tended to solidify their rebellion. They set up a bank account and opened a post office box in Cleveland for correspondence [Ibid], apart from the government and discipline of the church. The schism was thus virtually set in motion in that meeting. They met again [across the river in Indiana] before and after the General Assembly in Louisville, Kentucky in July 1992, and made further progress toward their expectations. Thereafter they convened meetings [against the counsel and pleadings of their overseers] in Jonesboro, Arkansas [October 1992] and Bessemer, Alabama [January 1993] enroute to their inevitable conclusion. After several admonitions, the General Overseer wrote a firm letter warning ministers that their credentials with the church were in jeopardy if they pursued their rebellious course. This letter was difiantly published and contradicted in *The Evening Light*, January 1993, 4-5. During the Jonesboro meeting they agreed to begin their publication of *The Evening Light*. This paper served as an organ to magnify their views and to "draw away disciples" from the discipline and order of the church. The monthly publication was replete with misinformation and often vilified the new administration and other ministers. It accused the church of apostasy, and excited passions that paved the way for the forthcoming schism.

[338]See notes 216-224.

[339]Several books and papers written by the present writer[e.g., "Quakerism and Frank W. Sandford: Major Influences that Transformed A. J. Tomlinson and the Church of God," and **The Nature of the Church**, WWPH, 1989] were denounced by The Concerned Group for not maintaining traditional interpretations in regard to Tomlinson's experience on Burger Mountain and the traditional claim that the Church of God of Prophecy was the exclusive body of Christ. E. Roger Ammons, for example, took issue with the writer's book, **The Nature of the Church**, insisting that the Church of God of Prophecy was exclusively God's church and predestined to be perfected and presented to Christ as His spotless bride [paper presented to the Questions and Subjects Committee, August 8, 1990]. During the Assembly in 1992 the writer agreed to meet with a delegation from this group before The Counseling Committee regarding their charges. Robert J. Pruitt and E. Roger Ammons were leaders in the group. [One member of the group suggested that the writer's license be revoked]. But after a short session the meeting was dismissed. It was realized that the church was at an *impasse* between static and traditional points of view, and new and dynamic points of view. The Concerned Group was locked into Tomlinson's revised historical interpretation that began in 1939 [see notes 216-224]. Ironically, some of the men who insisted that the Church of God of Prophecy was God's

exclusive church and predestined to be perfected, later recanted and formed a separate body in order to perpetuate the notion that they themselves represented exclusively God's church. Pruitt noted in an interview with the *Cleveland Daily Banner* that the schism "is based entirely on objections to 'deviations' by the present leadership from the original teachings and revelation of the Church of God of Prophecy" [Corky Hoover, "Group splits from church, elects Pruitt," *Cleveland Daily Banner*, July 27, 1993].

[340]"The Concerned For Bible Doctrine," *The Evening Light*, March 1993, 3-4.

[341]Robert J. Pruitt was included. His license was revoked [after refusing counsel from his ruling elders] for becoming "party to a lawsuit against the church" [Corky Hoover, "Groups splits," *Cleveland Daily Banner*, July 27, 1993]; interviews with Billy D. Murray Sr., General Overseer; Eugene Weakley, State Overseer of Tennessee; Sam Clements, State Overseer of Arkansas.

[342]This move had been developing since Murray's selection in 1990 [see notes 317-318, 329]. The seed for its conception had been planted in the presbytery meeting itself. Thereafter it developed as an embryo in the womb of the church. It was nourished by *The Evening Light* publications beginning in Novemeber 1992 and the Jonesboro and Bessemer meetings [see note 347]. It was further encouraged by three "messages in tongues" given out at the South Cleveland church on February 3, April 11, 25, 1993, which were interpreted as a divine call "to come out" of the Church of God of Prophecy and form a separate organization [*The Evening Light*, June 1993, 3-6]. But the schism was not born until the so-called Solemn Assembly in Chattanooga in July 23-25, 1993. In this meeting the group selected Robert J. Pruitt to be their General Overseer and set up a central office in his house and a post office box in Charleston near Cleveland ["A New Beginning," *The Evening Light*, August 1993, 1-4; Corky Hoover, "Group splits," *Cleveland Daily Banner*, July 27, 1993].

[343]Pruitt admitted to Corky Hoover, Executive Editor of the *Cleveland Daily Banner*, that "he became party to a lawsuit against the church" [July 27, 1993]. Thereafter he wrote

several messages in *The Evening Light* [e.g., "Divided We Stand," December 1992, 1-2; "Creeping Apostasy," February 1993,1-2; "Profaning The Covenant," March 1993,11-12; "Their Pernicious Ways," May 1993, 13;"I Am Not Ashamed," June 1993, 13-15] that encouraged the inevitable schism.

[344]Ibid; and see R. O. Covey, "Called to be 'THE CHURCH OF GOD,' " *The Evening Light*, August 1993, 11-12. It is noteworthy that J. L. Scott and his followers [1919], A. J. Tomlinson and his followers [1923], Homer A. Tomlinson and his followers [1943], Grady R. Kent and his followers [1957], and Robert J. Pruitt and his followers [1993], all made the same basic claim; namely, that the church had apostatized, and that they were reforming to perpetuate the original teachings; and thus they were exclusively the true church.

[345]The estimates varied between 1800 and 3000 members and 75 and 125 ministers. The highest figures represented only about one percent of the church. Pruitt claimed about 23 congregations in an interview to the *Cleveland Daily Banner* after the so-called Solemn Assembly in July 1993 [Corky Hoover, "Group splits," July 27, 1993]. This was representative of less than one-half of one percent of the church's 5500 congregations.

[346]Once the contention fulfilled itself in a divorce, the small faction became unaccountable for its gossip and accusations and was free to say all manner of evil against the "apostate" Church of God of Prophecy [particularly its leaders]. This was even encouraged in order to proselytize the "good ministers and members" who were now perceived to be in the clutches of "Babylon" [See "Proclamation," *The Evening Light*, August 1993, 2-4; Lois Lawrence, "The Return to Babylon," Ibid, 7].

[347]A suit was filed also over rights to use the Church flag [this suit is still pending the court's ruling].

[348]Corky Hoover, "Group splits," *Cleveland Daily Banner*, July 27, 1993.

[349]This system was initiated with the "Big Business Program" in 1928 [see note 214]. It was developed to cope with the depression in the late 1920s and 1930s and thereafter was perpetuated, though its original purpose had been served.

[350]Complaints had been increasing for years on the field against the inbalance between local churches and General Headquarters; but the executive administration would not budge to modify the system. It was another one of those changes that Tomlinson put on hold in order to avoid more hassel than necessary before he resigned. The problem was taken up by Murray soon after he assumed office. He noted, "We are being forced to review at once the ministry and mission of General Headquarters. Of one thing I am certain— the local church is the location of spiritual thrust as we evangelize the world and as we nurture and disciple believers. Therefore, the function of our headquarters operation is to serve the local churches..." ["A Heartfelt Address," 4].

[351]Ibid, 3-4.

[352]See Questions and Subject Committee Report, Section 3, *Minutes of the Eighty-Sixth Annual Assembly*, 1991, 110. This was another decision that upset a number of ministers and members, for Cleveland had been held as a sacred place for the Church of God since A. J. Tomlinson's annual address in 1935. Moreover, the financial crisis seemed to necessitate "an every-other-year Assembly" [an Assembly event averaged $450,000.00] rather than the traditional annual event, and so was recommended by the Committee [Ibid]. This was a disruption of a tradition that started with the first Assembly in 1906.

[353]The Ways and Means Committee Report, *Minutes of the Eighty- Sixth Assembly*, 1992, 55-62.

[354]The Ways and Means Committee Report called for radical reform that effected every department of the church [See *Minutes of the Eighty-Eighth Assembly*, 1994, 69-76].

[355]Ibid.

[356]Ibid, 77; and see Finance and Stewardship Committee Report, *Minutes of the Eighty-Ninth Assembly,* 1996, 43-48; and "Present Financial System" [Ibid, 157-161].

[357]The Committee produced a thirty-three page report published under the title, *Study of the Office of General Overseer,* 1991 [WHPC].

[358]Questions and Subjects Committee Report, Section 2, *Minutes of the Eighty-Eighth Assembly,* 1994, 53-59.

[359]The meeting convened at the Tomlinson College campus, August 14-19, 1997.

[360]See report of the presbytery meeting in the *White Wing Messenger* ["Selection of the General Presbyters," September 27, 1997, 6-7]. This report was modified to avoid the strong disagreements expressed in the meeting, particularly in regard to two of the presbyters who are to reside in Cleveland [many left the meeting dissatisfied with the process of selection]; see also "Understanding Plurality" [Ibid, 8-9] and the General Overseer's address— "Doing Nothing of Ourselves"—presented to the presbytery at the beginning of the meeting [Ibid, 4-5].

The Doctrine

Foreword

At the risk of making unworthy comparisons, it is interesting to note that Platonists are so designated because of their understanding and commitment to the doctrine of Platonism. Similarly Marxists are well prepared to defend and discuss the system of Marxism. Strikingly, however, the modern day Christian seems content to place less importance on the essential doctrines of the Faith, justified in part by the oft made claim that "*doctrine divides.*" True that as followers of our Lord, we are called to live in relationship with Him in a way that an abstract system of universal truths simply does not reproduce what is really involved. However, the living Christ does not call for a mystical union, that is predicated on a one-time salvation experience, nor does He even call for a literal imitation. But He does call for practical, personal discipleship.

In a very real sense, our Lord Jesus does not intend that His followers should separate His teachings (doctrine) from His person. The form of radical discipleship that followers of our Lord must experience calls for a life that is transformed from the roots upward, a new basic attitude, a different scale of values, a radical rethinking and returning (*metanoia*) of the whole man. Why then do we Christians make an issue of doctrine? One reason would have to be the fact that as a community—the church—the basis of our fellowship (*koinonia*) and the ability to defend the gospel is both lifestyle and knowledge related. In this respect, the church is faced with the same challenge today as in the first century. The message of the church cannot solely be communicated or deduced from its doctrines, but emerge in a very concrete way out of a complex tension between intellectual reflection and immediate involvement.

The apostle Paul made his case for the place of "sound doctrine" in the church when he stated the qualifications for those who would serve as bishops in the church. Among other things, Paul said to Titus that a bishop should be a man, ". . . holding fast the faithful word as he has been taught, that he may be able, by sound doctrine, both to exhort and convict those who contradict" (Titus 1:9 NKJV). Interesting that Paul often made mention of the need for doctrine, not so much to convict sinners of the truth, but as a defense for those within the Christian community—the church—who would oppose apostolic truth.

In this study, the student will explore the fundamental truths that are considered of primary importance to the understanding of the Church of God of Prophecy as a corporeal body of people. While we recognize that it is the whole Bible that dictates and defines the life of the Christian, giving prominence to certain teaching allows the church to fully recognize and embrace the truths that have long been part of the great tradition of the church. In addition, members who wish to examine and reflect on the basis of their faith in Christ, should be able to confidently make use of this material for that purpose. At the same time, accepting this discipleship challenge should make it easier for all members to ". . . always be ready to give a defense to everyone who asks you a reason for the hope that is in you, with meekness and fear" (1 Peter 3:15 NKJV). The believer's task is to know well the truths of the faith and to prepare to present them in a persuasive fashion.

This lesson should be viewed as a first step in the crucial task of assimilating elements of truth, while striving to cultivate a dynamic relationship with the One who is "the way, the truth, and the life." In the process, I believe it will not only help us to be more complete Christians, but also to become more committed members of the Church of God of Prophecy, where these truths are still held to be unshakable fundamentals of the Faith.

Introduction

From a New Testament perspective, the word *doctrine* in Greek comes from *didache* and *didaskalia* that are derived form the root "to teach," implying the act of teaching or the content of that which is taught. Thus, doctrine has become synonymous with the basic body of Christian teaching or understanding (2 Timothy 3:16). In practice, we may regard Christian doctrine as those essential teachings that are to be handed on through instruction and proclamation. **The doctrine of the Church of God of Prophecy is an agreed corporate expression of an authoritative interpretation of Scripture based on theological themes.**

The need for consistent teaching as perhaps the chief means of acquainting members with the doctrine of the church is probably more of an imperative today than at anytime in the past. One reason is the desire shared by many pastors to make their preaching more directly related to the gospel message, in order for it to have a strong appeal to the unsaved. This means that Sunday morning messages that deal largely with theological themes are somehow seen as missing the mark. How then are members of the church to be instructed and reminded of the truth and lifestyle requirements of the Faith "once delivered"?

Without loseing the opportunity to share the gospel at the most opportune time in the church schedule, pastors are challenged at the same time to ensure members of the church are well-grounded in the doctrine of the church. This may call for a special effort to teach and to discuss this lesson periodically. The aim would be to ensure both the clarity of scriptural interpretation, and the application in the particular context in which members live. We need teachers who are able to offer a clear and connected interpretation of church doctrine, and by so doing, present a coherent explication of what the members should believe and how they should behave.

We know that God and His Word remain consistent and unchanging. However, there is an ever-present need to ensure the accuracy of that which is handed on, and to assist with the understanding and relevance to the cultural context in which it must be lived. Our teaching of church doctrine quite likely will have to be stated anew for each generation in the language that generation speaks. The heart of doctrine remains a systematic examination of the content of the relationship which God in Christ has entered into with us. It is important that every member of the church is given the opportunity to come to terms the doctrine of the Church of God of Prophecy in the knowledge that the time in which we live is characterized by doctrinal compromise and indifference.

The Doctrine of the Church of God of Prophecy

Learning Goals and Objectives:

The individual will demonstrate an understanding of the *doctrine* of the Church of God of Prophecy by:

- explaining the significance of the trinitarian nature of God and the divinity of Christ.

- explaining the position of the Church of God of Prophecy regarding salvation, including defining conviction, justification, regeneration, born-again, repentance, and conversion.

- explaining the position of the Church of God of Prophecy on sanctification.

- discussing the significance of holiness of life including its relevance to such things as sexual behavior, marriage and family relationships, social life, oaths, tithing and giving, and restitution.

- describing the role of the Holy Spirit in the life of the believer, including the nature of Holy Spirit baptism, the role of speaking in tongues, the nature and functions of the gifts of the Spirit, and the significance of the fruit of the Spirit.

- describing the significance of the New Testament ordinances of the Lord's supper, feet-washing, and water baptism and identifying the conditions under which they are observed.

- explaining the nature, purpose, and function of the church.

- explaining the position of the Church of God of Prophecy regarding the last things, including the significance of the premillenial second coming of Christ, the resurrection of the dead, and eternal rewards.

The Triune God

Unit Two

Objective: The student will demonstrate an understanding of the _doctrine_ of the Church of God of Prophecy by explaining the significance of the trinitarian nature of God and the divinity of Christ.

Raymond M. Pruitt, _Fundamentals of the Faith_, pp. 95-98, 187-193

Having examined the reality of God's existence, and what He is like in His essence and in His manifestation of Himself through His divine attributes, we must now show what the church means when it defines the Trinity "as the union of three Persons—the Father, the Son, and the Holy Ghost in one Godhead."[1]

While the term "trinity" is not found in the Scriptures, the doctrine of the tri-unity of God which designates, is clearly implied throughout the Bible.

Through the induction of biblical passages dealing with the Godhead, we are forced to admit that the One indivisible God eternally exists in three Persons or Subsistences, and that these Subsistences have one and the same nature. How one substance can at the same time exist in three intelligent subsistences which are distinct from each other, and not merely three modes of manifestation, is not something which reason could teach us. This truth transcends reason. We have this from revelation, but no one understands it; we believe and teach it because the Bible teaches it, not because we understand it.

Nowhere does the Bible teach that truth is easy to understand. Some of the heretical teachings regarding the Trinity are easier to understand than the scriptural teachings. In this, Richard Hooker's words are to the point: "Heresy is more plain than true, whereas right belief is more than plain."

As we attempt to organize what the Bible teaches regarding the unity and the trinity of God into a systematic approach to understanding, we are thankful for what God has revealed regarding His triune nature, all the while knowing that we still have only a glimpse of what He actually is.

The Unity and Simplicity of God

By the unity of God is meant that there is but one God and that He is undivided and indivisible in His essence. Man is a compound of spirit and matter and lacks the simplicity which belongs to God alone. By the simplicity of God we mean that He is not composed of parts.

The Old Testament teaches that the divine nature is undivided and indivisible (Deuteronomy 6:4; 4:35, 39; Exodus 20:3; 1 Kings 8:60; Isaiah 45:5, 6; Zechariah 14:9; etc.). Likewise the New Testament contains definite confirmations of His unity (Mark 12:29-32; John 17:3; 1 Corinthians 8:4-6; Galatians 3:20; 1 Timothy 2:5; James 2:19; etc.). But the unity of God is not the unity of a stone which cannot exercise self-knowledge or self-consciousness, and cannot act in relation to itself, or to other existences. Nor does it mean that God the Father is the sole Deity, and that the Son and the Holy Ghost are subordinate members of a heavenly corporation called the Godhead.

The Trinity of God

While there is only one Divine Substance, there are three Persons of that one substance, co-equal, and co-eternal—the Father, the Son, and the Holy Ghost. This does not infer three Gods, but three eternal distinctions of the one substance of God. To say that they are three Gods would be *tritheism*, which denies the real unity of the essence of God and sets forth three Gods, whose unity consists in nothing more than an agreement in purpose and methodology. Some tritheists like to present the Godhead as a kind of family, with "God" as the family name, and each of the Persons as members of the one family, but each having a different first name. This is totally fallacious since it divides the substance into parts, destroys the simplicity of God's nature, and makes God something other than the Persons who comprise the Godhead. While the whole undivided essence of God belongs equally to each of the three Persons, "the Father is not the Trinity, nor the Son the Trinity, nor the Spirit the Trinity; but whenever each is singly spoken of, then they are not spoken of as three, in the plural number, but one, the Trinity itself" (Augustine).[2]

Throughout the history of Christian doctrine, many formal statements have been written setting forth the scriptural doctrine of the Trinity. Here we give one of the older and better known statements, followed by one more recently adopted by our General Assembly:

We worship "one God in Trinity, and Trinity in Unity, neither confounding the Persons nor separating the substance. The person of the Father is one, of the Son another, of the Holy Spirit another. But the Divinity of the Father, Son, and Spirit is one . . . all the three Persons are co-eternal, and co-equal, so that in all things both a trinity in unity and a unity in trinity is to be worshiped" (Athanasian Creed).[3] "The Son has always existed, but . . . He is not the Father. The Holy Ghost is a distinct person with all the attributes of God, yet He is neither the Father nor the Son."[4]

The doctrine of the Trinity is not the unity of parts, which make up a single composition, as the body, soul, and spirit of man does, "for God is a simple and uncompounded Spirit."[5]

THE TWO NATURES OF CHRIST

In this study we will consider how both the human nature and the divine nature are united in the one Person of our Lord Jesus Christ. The teaching of Scripture on this great mystery is aptly summed up in the statement of the Council of Chalcedon (A.D. 451), which declares the Person of Christ "to be acknowledged in two natures, inconfusedly, unchangeably, inseparably; the distinctions of the natures being in no wise taken away by the union, but rather the property of each nature being preserved, and concurring in one Person and one Subsistence, not parted or divided into two persons."[6]

Another helpful and descriptive statement is taken from the second article of the church of England: "The Son, which is the Word of the Father, begotten from everlasting of the Father, the very and eternal God, and of one Substance with the Father, took man's nature in the womb of the blessed virgin of her substance: so that two whole and perfect natures, that is to say, the Godhead and the manhood were joined together in one Person, never to be divided, whereof is one Christ, very God and very man."[7]

The Bible does not tell us how God and man became one Person in Jesus Christ; it simply proclaims who Jesus is without marshaling arguments and proofs of how He came to be. We approach the mystery with awe and reverence for Him who is the express "image of the invisible God" (Colossians 1:15; Hebrews 1:3), and who at the same time is "the man Christ Jesus" (1 Timothy 2:5).

The Deity of Christ

The importance of the doctrine of the deity of Christ cannot be overestimated, because if He is not God incarnate, then we have no Saviour, and Christianity is a religion without hope. The entire plan of salvation is founded upon His being very God manifest in the flesh. Deny this, and at best, Jesus would only be a prophet, but He could not be a Saviour. So great is our alienation from God, through the awful sinfulness of sin, that only the divine sinless Son of God could reconcile us. Other religions are founded upon the teachings of their founders. Buddha (563-484 B.C.), Confucius (551-478 B.C.), and Mohammed (A.D. 570-632) are important to their followers because of what they taught. But Christianity goes beyond the teachings of Jesus (which are complete and perfect in every respect) to find its foundation in the Person of the Lord Jesus Christ.

He is recognized as God. John 1:1, "The Word was God"; Hebrews 1:8, "Unto the Son he saith, Thy throne, O God, is for ever"; John 1:18, "The only begotten Son" "a great mass of ancient evidence" supports the translation of this clause as "the only begotten God"—in other words, the original Greek attributes deity to Christ in this statement,[8] John 20:28, "My Lord and my God" (Thomas was making a pointed confession of faith here, not using the name of God in vain as an expression of his wide-eyed astonishment. The fact that Jesus accepted his statement, and did not charge him with taking the name of God in vain, is tantamount to asserting His deity); Romans 9:5, "God blessed forever"; Titus 2:13, "The great God and our Saviour Jesus Christ"; 1 John 5:20, "Even in His Son Jesus Christ. This is the true God."

He is recognized as the Son of God. A Bible concordance will give a number of references to this title (Matthew 16:16, 17; 3:29; 14:33; Mark 1:1; 14:61; Luke 1:35; 4:41; John 5:25; 10:36; 11:4; 20:28). He was the only eternally begotten Son, not just a son. In one sense, to "as many as received him, to them gave he power to become the sons of God" (John 1:12), but this is in the moral and spiritual sense. Christ's Sonship is unique in its essence. It denotes His singular and transcendent relationship with the Father.

The Jews understood His claim when they "sought the more to kill him, because he . . . said . . . that God was His Father, making Himself equal with God" (John 5:18). He has always been the Son from eternity; there was never a time when He was not the Son of God.

He is recognized as Lord. See Acts 4:33; 16:31; Luke 2:11; Acts 9:17; Matthew 22: 43-45. As it had reference to Christ, the term "Lord" denoted His deity (Matthew 7:21, 22; Luke 1:43; John 20:28; Acts 16:31; 1 Corinthians 12:3; Philippians 2:11).

He is worshiped and worship is accepted by Him (Luke 5:8; Matthew 14:33; 15:25; 28:9; 1 Corinthians 1:2). Since only God is to be worshiped (Exodus 34:14 and Matthew 4:10), angels and devout men rejected the worship rendered to them (Acts 10:25, 26; Revelations 19:10; 22:8, 9), but Christ accepted it; therefore, by accepting worship He acknowledged that He is God. If He were not God, He would have been guilty of blasphemy. Not only does He accept worship, the Scriptures enjoin us to worship Him. Thiessen reminds us, "If He is not God, He is a deceiver or is self-deceived, and, in either case, if He is not God, He is not good (*Christus, si non Deus, non bonus*)."[9]

The Humanity of Christ

The scriptural teaching concerning Christ's humanity. The Scriptures abound with references to His humanity. In His humanity, He is like us in every way, except that He is without sin.

    a. He was born of a woman (Matthew 1:18; 2:11; 12:47; 13:55; John 1:14; 2:1; Acts 13:23; Romans 1:3; Galatians 4:4).

b. His human nature was thoroughly consistent with ours in that He hungered (Matthew 4:2); He thirsted (John 19:28); He grew weary (John 4:6); He felt pain in the garden and on the cross; He died and was buried (Matthew 27: 33-66; Mark 15:22-47; Luke 22:44; 23:44; 23:26; John 19: 16-42).

c. He was subject to the laws of human development (Luke 2:40, 46, 52).

d. He had a human soul (John 12:27; Matthew 26:38) and spirit (Luke 23:46; 10:21).

The incarnation a true human nature. By His incarnation Christ took on true human nature. He not only came to us, but He became one with us (Hebrews 2:11). The fact that He also possessed divine properties, or attributes, does not distract from His humanity, or his normal human development. His human nature was true and complete, without any impairments or additions to its essential qualities.

Two natures, one Person. It is difficult for human reason to understand, or to explain how there could be two perfect natures in but one true Person. The Bible calls it a mystery (Colossians 2:2, 3), and notes that it can be known only through divine revelation (Matthew 11:27). Since there is no other person like Him, we have no way of basing our study upon something known, and then moving toward an understanding of the unknown. Revelation according to the Scriptures is the only source of this knowledge.

Some errors to be avoided. Care should be taken not to fall into the errors of some who have sought to explain the union of the two natures through reason alone.

a. It is not a union similar to the marriage of a man and a woman, for in that relationship, both parties continue to be two persons. They are one flesh, but two persons.

b. Nor can it be likened to the relationship of believers who are united to Christ, for having Christ does not make us God, nor is He made human because we dwell in Him.

c. Neither did the two natures combine so as to form a third nature, as water and salt mixed together results in a third element, brine. The Eutychians, named after Eutyches, abbot of Constantinople in the fifth century A.D., fell into the error of supposing that the human nature Christ was transformed into the divine nature by absorption, so that there was only one nature in the Incarnation.

The mystery of the doctrine. The union of the two natures in the one Person of Christ is one of the greatest mysteries of our faith. According to the Bible, it was necessary that He be God and man at the same time, but without mixing or fusing the two natures into one nature. Because of its mystery, next to the doctrine of the Trinity, there is no other doctrine that has given more rise to more heresies than the doctrine of the incarnation of Christ.

The Necessity of the Two Natures of Christ

The necessity of His humanity. Since man was the transgressor, man must pay the penalty for his sin. Unless Christ became very man by taking on our true nature, along with all the sinless infirmities and limitations, He could not have taken our place in paying the penalty for our sin, since He would not have been one with us. It was also necessary that He be a sinless man who "was in all points tempted like as we are, yet without sin" (Hebrews 7:25, 26). Salvation can come only through a truly human Mediator, who has been where we are and was victorious over all temptations to sin (Hebrews 2:17, 18; 4:15; 5:2); only He could offer a sacrifice of Himself which would be accepted by a holy God for sinful man (Romans 5:17, 18).

The necessity of His deity. In the economy of God, it was also essential that the Redeemer be very God, for God alone is adequate to cope with our need. God alone could perfectly reveal Himself to man by appearing Himself among them. God alone could reconcile men to Himself (John 1:12), for no man could bridge that gap. It was essential that He be God so that He might offer a sacrifice of infinite value, and render perfect obedience to the law of God; so that He might through His sacrifice effect redemption for those who believe on Him, thus freeing them from the curse of the law, so that He might bring believers all the abundance of His finished work. No man could qualify to pay the penalty of sin, nor render perfect obedience to God. Man can and does bear the wrath of God against sin (except where the grace of God has delivered men from the law of sin and death), but no man can bear the wrath of God in such a way as to open up a way of escape through that very suffering (Psalms 22:29; 49:7-10; 130:3, 4).

The Character of Christ

Not only is Christ uniquely alone in the nature of His relationship to man and to God, He is also alone in His character. When we look upon Him, we feel compelled to say with Isaiah, "Woe is me! for I am undone; because I am a man of unclean lips, and I dwell in the midst of a people of unclean lips: for mine eyes have seen the King, the Lord of hosts" (Isaiah 6:5). The wonder of sanctification is that He imparts His righteousness to those who abandon themselves wholly to Him in total faith and full surrender.

His holiness. He is absolutely holy (Luke 1:35; Acts 2:27; 3:14; 4:27). The prince of this world has nothing in Him (John 14:30). He was "without sin" (Hebrews 4:15), and "separate from sinners" (Hebrews 7:26). He "did no sin, neither was guile found in His mouth" (1 Peter 2:22, 23).

His love. He was perfect in love, both toward men (Ephesians 3:18; Matthew 11:19; Mark 10:21; John 10:11; 13:1; 15:13; Romans 5:8; 8:37-39; Ephesians 5:2, 25) and toward God (John 14:31).

His humility. He was humble, meek, and lowly (Philippians 2:5-8) and became poor for our sake (2 Corinthians 8:9; 10:6; Luke 2:7; 9:58; Matthew 11:19, 29: 17:27; 20:28; 27:57-60).

His prayer life. He prayed much (Matthew 14:23; Mark 1:35; Luke 6:12; Hebrews 5:7).

His dedication. He was always devoted to His work (see Matthew 8:16; Mark 1:35; Luke 6:12; John 3:2; 5:17; 8:2; 9:4). In His work, He was courageous (John 2:14-17; 19:10, 11), thorough (Matthew 11:19), and tactful (John 4:7-30).

He was perfect in the midst of an imperfect world. He had an authority that commanded attention. He moved in the circle of everyday life and selected His disciples from the lowly.

He was tempted, but never yielded. He was seen in all situations and sustained the same consistent character throughout. He finished the work given Him to do. In His relation to women He combined purity with familiarity and tenderness. He represented unbroken unity and communion with God. He was a man, not of inactive contemplation, but of practical activity. He arose above all prejudices and bigotries. He was free from one-sidedness, not a man of one idea, nor any one temperament. His virtue was healthy, manly, vigorous, yet genial, social, and winning. His qualities were in perfect balance; zeal never degenerating into passion, childish innocence combined with manly strength, fearless courage with wise caution. He was complete in suffering. He exalted forgiveness and submission. He bore pain and death superhumanly, in a divine glory of spirit, with a commanding grandeur and majesty. He set forth His amazing claims as self-evident truths. He is an unsolvable problem unless He is the Son of God.[10]

The Triune God

Unit Two

Objective: The individual will demonstrate an understanding of the *doctrine* of the Church of God of Prophecy by explaining the position of the Church of God of Prophecy regarding salvation, including defining conviction, justification, regeneration, born-again, repentance, and conversion.

James Stone, *The Church of God of Prophecy History and Polity*, pp. 232-235

When man comes face to face with the eternal decision of salvation which has been wrought by the Word and the Spirit of God, he will either repent or be damned. *Conviction*, the revelation that the God of justice and love is calling the sinner, will bring a man to his knees of repentance or to his feet of defiance. The call of God to the sinner is the beginning of the spiritual experiences.

Repentance, the change wrought in the life of a sinner which causes him to turn from sin, is essential to salvation. True repentance will involve three basic concerns. The sinner will intellectually come to the knowledge that he stands guilty, corrupt, and offensive before a holy God. Romans 3:20 indicates that this element of repentance is coming to "the knowledge of sin."

Repentance is more than just the realization that an individual "is conscious of his guilt as a sinner in the presence of God." There is an emotional concern also in true repentance. The sinner, realizing his guiltiness, corruptiveness, and offensiveness before a holy God must come to "hate his ways." If he does not, then he merely fears punishment, but has no hatred of sin. Second Corinthians 7:9 illustrates this element of repentance: "Now I rejoice, not that ye were made sorry, but that ye sorrowed to repentance: for ye were made sorry after a godly manner."

Repentance is more than just coming to the intellectual knowledge of the wages of sin, and more than just being sorrowful for the ways of sins; it is also concern with an act of will. After the sinner realizes he stands guilty, corrupt, and offensive before a holy God, and he "made sorry after a godly manner," he must purpose in his will to turn away from sin. If he does not turn from his guilty, sorrowful ways, then he has only "the sorrow of the world [which] worketh death" (2 Corinthians 7:10). True repentance will bring a sinner to the realization that he stands guilty before God, to godly sorrow and hatred of sins because of its effect upon his life and to purposely turn from sin. Repentance brings the sinner, because of his knowledge of sin, his godly sorrow and his turning from sin, to the seeking of forgiveness so that he might be ultimately justified and sanctified.

Repentance prepares the sinner for *justification*. Repentance does not pardon or justify the sinner "but when he comes to Jesus with a humble and contrite spirit and confesses his sins and is willing to forsake sin" he is ready to be justified.[11] After he is justified, the sinner stands before God freed from the consequences of guilt and judgment of sin.

Just as the sinner's sins were imputed to Jesus Christ at the cross, the righteousness of Jesus Christ can now be imputed to the sinner. Justification wrought by faith in the blood of Jesus Christ is a judicial act of God. God forgives the sins of the sinner and declares him to be righteous on the basis of the righteousness of Jesus Christ, and frees him from all guilt and judgment that he deserved as a sinner.

Justification involves the forgiveness of sin and the restoring of the sinner to divine favor. Romans 4:5-8 illustrates the first point: "But to him that worketh not, but believeth on him that justifieth the ungodly, his faith is counted for righteousness. Even as David also describeth the blessedness of the man, unto whom God imputeth righteousness without works, Saying, Blessed are they whose iniquities are forgiven, and whose sins are covered. Blessed is the man to whom the Lord will not impute sin."

Romans 5:1, 2 indicates the latter point: "Therefore being justified by faith, we have peace with God through our Lord Jesus Christ: By whom also we have access by faith into this grace wherein we stand, and rejoice in hope of the glory of God."

Regeneration is wrought by an act of God through the Word and the Spirit whereby the seed of the new life is implanted in man. The new creature in Christ, through regeneration and the new birth, is changed from the old creature. These experiences affect the whole man—intellectually, emotionally, and morally. As far as the experience, regeneration and the new birth are the same.[12]

Sanctification is an act of God through the Word and the Spirit whereby "the 'old man' (man's corruptive condition) is completely eradicated by the blood of Jesus Christ."[13] The sanctified believer is free from the law of sin and death. In the act of justification the sinner has his personal transgressions forgiven; whereas, in the act of sanctification the pollution of sin which causes man to transgress is removed.

Significance of Holiness of Life

Unit Two

Objective: The individual will demonstrate an understanding of the *doctrine* of the Church of God of
Prophecy by discussing the significance of holiness of life
including its relevance to such things as sexual behavior,
marriage and family relationships, social life, oaths,
tithing and giving, and restitution.

James Stone, *The Church of God of Prophecy History
and Polity*, pp. 236, 245, 246, 249-257

Holiness, as one of the teachings of the church, "refers to a
condition or a way of life."[14] The writer of Hebrews proclaims,
"Follow peace with all men, and holiness, without which no
man shall see the Lord" (Hebrews 12:14). The word "holiness"
is translated from the Greek word *hagiasmos* (hag-ee- as-mos).
Hagiasmos is defined as "santification, essential purity."[15]

When the Church of God states that holiness is a teaching
of the church, the church is simply implying that the members of the church are encouraged to live a life of holiness—
a life that is characterized by "cleanliness of heart," freedom
from sin, the state of being holy or dedicated and consecrated to the will of God, and a holiness that can only come from
an act of God through the ministry of the Word and the
Spirit. Holiness, which is nothing more or nothing less than
purity of heart and life, is made possible by the experience of
sanctification.[16]

The practice of *paying tithes* and *giving offerings* is consistent with the entire Bible. Anyone who fails to pay their tithes
and give in offerings is living a life that is not in harmony
with the Word of God. Indeed, Jesus, the living Word, gave
His blessings to tithe-paying (Matthew 23:23).

The giving of tithes can be traced from Abraham to the present day. The writer of Hebrews (7:2) refers to Abraham giving a "tenth part of all" to Melchizedek. Genesis 14:20 gives the actual account: "and he gave him tithes of all." Abraham "lived and paid tithes at least four hundred years before the Law."[17]

In Genesis 28:22 when Jacob experienced the vision of the ladder, he made a vow to God: ". . . and all that thou shalt give me I will surely give the tenth unto thee." Jacob paid tithes of all that was given to him from God.

When Christ came fulfilling the law he sanctioned the paying of tithes (Matthew 23:23). The paying of tithes would no longer be compulsory, but the laws of God written on the hearts of men by Christ would compel them to be faithful to God's financial plan. The paying of one-tenth of the increase into the church treasury has become the established practice of the last days Church of God.

In addition to paying tithes, each member of the church should support the plan of God by offerings. The basic differences between tithing and giving of offerings are: tithes are a specific amount (a tenth), whereas, offerings are determined by the giver; tithes are restricted to the use of the ministry, whereas offerings can be used for any purpose.[18] Paul emphasizes the correctness in giving: "But this I say, He which soweth sparingly shall reap also sparingly; and he which soweth bountifully shall reap also bountifully. Every man according as he purposeth in his heart, so let him give; not grudgingly, or of necessity: for God loveth a cheerful giver. And God is able to make all grace abound toward you; that ye, always having all sufficiency in all things, may abound to every good work: (As it is written, He hath dispersed abroad; he hath given to the poor: his righteousness remaineth forever)" (2 Corinthians 9:6-9).

The seventeenth teaching of the church made prominent is *"restitution where possible."* When it is possible, wrongs committed must be made right. The basis for this belief is found in the conversation between Jesus and Zacchaeus (Luke 19:8, 9) and certain other key verses (Matthew 3:8; Romans 13:8).[19] Restitution is a natural by-product of salvation.[20] One of the "fruits meet for repentance" (Matthew 3:8) is the desire to make things right after truly becoming godly sorrowful for wrongs committed. "The act of giving back that which was wrongfully taken away" should be the desire born of every regenerated heart.

The New Testament not only teaches about the life to come, the last things, the Word of God also instructs us in living this life. Living in the grace dispensation the believers in Christ have certain freedoms that were not enjoyed by those living under the law or other religious systems.

In addition to the total freedom in Christ there are two specific teachings on Christian freedom made prominent by the Church of God. Those teachings are on *meats and drinks* and on the *Sabbath*.

Paul stated that in the latter times some would come teaching "and commanding to abstain from meat . . ." (1 Timothy 4:3). To which he stressed "every creature of God is good, and nothing to be refused, if it be received with thanksgiving" (1 Timothy 4:4). The church takes the same stand with Paul and with the rest of the Word of God. There is not any passage of the New Testament in regard to sin that "would indicate that [man is] to refrain from eating certain kinds of food."[21] With the exception of intoxicating beverages, the same can be said concerning drinks. "For the kingdom of God is not meat and drink; but righteousness, and peace, and joy in the Holy Ghost" (Romans 14:17).

There is, however, a caution from the Scripture that believers should not offend their brethren in the Lord. Peter stated, "As free, and not using your liberty for a cloak of maliciousness, but as the servants of God" (1 Peter 2:16). The Christian must exercise extreme caution lest he offend his brother. With this understanding it can be stated that the "New Testament makes no rigid rule as to what the Christian is to eat or drink."[22] The following Scriptures summarize the church's teaching on meats and drinks: "For one believeth that he may eat all things: another, who is weak, eateth herbs. Let not him that eateth despise him that eateth not; and let not him which eateth not judge him that eateth: for God hath received him . . . For the kingdom of God is not meat and drink" (Romans 14: 2, 3, 7).

The entire Word of God stands consistently against strong drink-alcoholic beverages which have an intoxicating effect upon the human body. The writer of Proverbs boldly proclaims, "Wine is a mocker, strong drink is raging: and whosoever is deceived thereby is not wise" (Proverbs 20:1). The writer again cries, "Who hath woe? who hath sorrow? who hath contentions? who hath babbling? who hath wounds without a cause? who hath redness of eyes? They that tarry long at the wine; they that go to seek mixed wine. Look not thou upon the wine when it is red, when it giveth his colour in the cup, when it moveth itself aright. At the last it biteth like a serpent, and stingeth like an adder" (Proverbs 23:29-32).

The New Testament adds to those warnings in Paul's discussion on the works of the flesh. Before Paul listed the works of the flesh, he stated that "the flesh lusteth against the Spirit, and the Spirit against the flesh: and these are contrary the one to the other" (Galatians 5:17). After he listed the works of the flesh he proclaimed "that they which do such things shall not inherit the kingdom of God" (Galatians 5:21). Paul says "the works of the flesh are manifest, which are these . . . drunkenness" (Galatians 5:21). Drunkenness is listed along with adultery, fornication, witchcraft, murders, and the evils of Satanic influence.

The Church of God recognizes the danger of alcoholic beverages and firmly takes a stand of *total abstinence*. Paul states, "What? know ye not that your body is the temple of the Holy Ghost which is in you, which ye have of God, and ye are not your own? For ye are bought with a price: therefore glorify God in your body, and in your spirit, which are God's" (1 Corinthians 6:19-20).

No child of God, when he realizes that his body is the temple of the Holy Ghost, will want to defile his body with strong drink. These are the reasons why total abstinence from all liquor and strong drink is a prominent teaching of the Church of God.

The church also takes a strong stand *against the use of tobacco, opium, morphine, and other narcotics.* The church "teaches against [these] being consumed or used to satisfy the carnal desires of man."[23] The same passages of Scripture from the New Testament that restrict the Christian from using strong drink also restrict the Christian from using these traps of Satan.

Paul again admonished the believer "Having therefore these promises, dearly beloved, let us cleanse ourselves from all filthiness of the flesh and spirit, perfecting holiness in the fear of God" (2 Corinthians 7:1). The church boldly stands upon the fact that believers "are called unto a life of holiness and there is no place in the life of a holy sanctified saint of God from superfluities of the flesh and things which do not contribute to the perfecting of holiness in the fear of God."[24] Ever since the Assembly of 1906, the church has stood against the use of tobacco.

The basic reason why the church teaches against the use to strong drink and tobacco is that it defiles the temple of God. The church understands that salvation is not based upon what a man eats or drinks (Romans 14:17); however, once a believer has accepted Jesus Christ, has been sanctified and has been filled with the Holy Ghost, he is challenged to live accordingly. Not because he is forced, but because there is such a law of love written on his heart, he is so inclined to live a life of "perfecting holiness in the fear of God."

Adornment—the Christian's use of adornment should be guided by the biblical principles of sobriety, modesty, submission, and self-discipline—Matthew 16a; 24; 1 Timothy 2:1-10; 1 Peter 3:17; John 2:16. Scripture explicitly teaches the use of adornment for occultic, lascivious, and idolatrous practices is prohibited (Acts 8:9; 13:6; 19:19; 1 Corinthians 5:10; 6:9; Galatians 5:19-21).

The next teaching of the church recognizes the Bible's command not to be "unequally yoked together" especially the "associations in which the believer is bound by oath with those who do not believe and against taking part with the unbelievers in their evil deeds."[25] Jesus prayed, "I pray not that thou shouldest take them out of the world, but that thou shouldest keep them from the evil." He went on to state, "They are not of the world, even as I am not of the world" (John 17:15, 16). The Christian is placed in a vicarious position. The believer must be in the world but not of the world. He must realize his responsibility to take the message of Christ to the whole world, which involves contact with people, but yet must not become too closely associated with that world he is trying to win.

Even though there is sometimes good accomplished through charity and assistance to the needy programs, the believer must use extreme caution not to become a part of any group that does anything in secret, especially those that "are of a nature that would prohibit a Christian from having fellowship with them."[26] As Paul states, "And have no fellowship with the unfruitful works of darkness, but rather reprove them, for it is a shame even to speak of those things which are done of them in secret" (Ephesians 5:11,12). He further adds, "For ye were sometimes darkness, but now are ye light in the Lord: walk as children of light" (Ephesians 5: 8). Finally, the church's teachings against belonging is summarized by Paul in 2 Corinthians 6:14, 17 and 18: "Be ye not unequally yoked together with unbelievers: for what fellowship hath righteousness with unrighteousness? and what communion hath light with darkness? Wherefore come out from among them, and be ye separate, saith the Lord, and touch not the unclean thing; and I will receive you, and will be a Father unto you, and ye shall be my sons and daughters, saith the Lord Almighty."

To become a member of a lodge usually requires the individual to "perform secret rites and ceremonies, use passwords, secret covenants, or a particular kind of handshake known only to the members of the organization."[27] This kind of secrecy goes strictly against the teachings of Jesus Christ. He said, "I spake openly to the world; I ever taught in the synagogue, and in the temple, whither the Jews always resort; and in secret have I said nothing" (John 18:20). Therefore, the church stands *against members belonging to lodges.*

An oath of allegiance is also usually required by the lodges of all their members. This, again, is taught against by the Scriptures. Jesus simply stated, "Swear not at all" (Matthew 5:34). James instructed the early church, "But above all things, my brethren, swear not, neither by heaven, neither by the earth, neither by any other oath: but let your yea be yea; and nay, nay; lest ye fall into condemnation" (James 5:12). Thus, the twenty-eighth teaching of the church made prominent is *against swearing.*

The Church of God firmly believes, "A child of God should not swear at all. He should not take an oath to become a member of any organization, neither should he take an oath to secure his word. He should not swear by the Lord, or by heaven or earth or any of His creation."

The last teaching made prominent by the church is *against the divorce and remarriage evil.* The Church of God primarily takes her stand upon this teaching from the words of Jesus. He stated, "For this cause shall a man leave his father and mother, and cleave to his wife; and they twain shall be one flesh: so then they are no more twain, but one flesh. What therefore God hath joined together, let not man put asunder" (Mark 10:7-9).

The background for this statement is quite interesting. The marriage bond, like in today's world, had almost been completely destroyed at the time of this statement by Jesus. The marriage bond and the home were in danger of collapsing.[28] A brief look at marriage from the vantage point of the Greeks, the Romans, and the Jews will illustrate this point.

To the Greeks, marriage meant little, if any, significant fidelity as far as the man was concerned. Infidelity for the men carried no stigma whatsoever. It was recognized as the accepted practice of life; on the other hand, the respectable married woman had to live a life of almost total seclusion. She had no social life nor could she even appear on the streets alone, and above all, she was held to the strictest code of purity. In summary, the Greeks "demanded the most moral purity" out of the women, and yet the men had "the utmost immoral license."[29]

To the Romans, marriage and the home were at one time the very crux of their entire life. The whole Roman way of life evolved around the home. The father was in complete power; the mother, unlike her Greek counterpart, participated in the full scheme of the marriage. Infidelity was held in contempt. Unfortunately, however, when Rome conquered Greece militarily, Greece, in turn, conquered Rome morally. By the second century before Christ, divorce became as common as marriage.[30]

To the Jews at the time of Christ the question of marriage and divorce was steeped in controversy. At one time the Jews, or at least their ancestors, had a very lofty ideal of marriage (Genesis 2:24). By the time of Christ, however, through Moses permitting divorce because of the hardness of the Israelites' hearts, the situation of marriage and divorce was hotly debated. There were two schools of thought concerning divorce. Deuteronomy 24:1 states, "When a man hath taken a wife and married her, and it comes to pass that she find no favor in his eyes, because he hath found some uncleanness in her" was interpreted by the strict school of Shammai as meaning only unchastity. The act of adultery was the only means by which a man could divorce his wife. On the other hand, the liberal school of Hillel interpreted that phrase to mean almost anything that man wanted it to mean. To them a man might divorce his wife for even the smallest of reasons, such as, not cooking his dinner to his fancy. It is not hard to ascertain which school of thought the people chose to accept. By the time of Jesus, divorce was becoming so easy, it was threatening the very institution of marriage.[31]

This was the reason why the question was asked Jesus concerning divorce in Mark 9. The Pharisees knew the controversy existed and wanted to draw Jesus into that debate. They knew He would offend some regardless of which school of thought He recommended. Jesus, however, shocked them with His profound statement that He was not taking either side of the divorce debate because from the beginning it was not so.

Jesus profoundly proclaimed, in the midst of the chaos of the Greek, the Roman, and the Jewish customs concerning marriage and divorce, the absolute ideal of marriage. "From the beginning of the creation God made them male and female . . . What therefore God hath joined together, let not man put asunder" (Mark 10:6, 9). Adam and Eve were to serve as the pattern for each married couple to come. When they are "joined together and become one flesh [they] will remain one flesh as long as they both shall live."[32] The Church of God has come to accept, along with the statements of Mark, (Mark 10:2-12), Luke, (Luke 16:18) and Paul, (Romans 7:2, 3; 1 Cor. 7:10, 11) that "when people marry they are married for life."[33]

Perhaps, one of the greatest difficulties of New Testament interpretation is the seemingly obvious disagreement between Matthew's statement of 19:9 (also 5:32) and the above-mentioned statements of Mark, Luke, and Paul. The clause stated by Jesus as recorded by Matthew, "except it be for fornication," has been the subject of as much debate in today's world as the clause "because he hath found some uncleanness in her" was in the Jewish world some two thousand years ago. The interpretation of just what fornication (*pornea*) means in the light of these two verses is difficult to ascertain from the works of the best Greek and New Testament scholars of today.

The Church of God, however, building upon the absolute ideal of marriage, has come to recognize the biblical truth that the state of fornication exists when one is unlawfully married to someone else's companion. The state of fornication, therefore, can be defined in the light of the biblical ideal of one man and one woman for one lifetime and in the context of the statement of Jesus as the condition whereby one has an unlawful wife. When a man is in the state of fornication, he may flee that sinful state by dissolving the unlawful union, and then he is free to marry his own wife.

When all of the Bible is taken together, the church stands firm with the words of Jesus. The absolute ideal of one man with one woman uniting in one marriage becoming one flesh and remaining that way as long as they both live, regardless of the action of any courts of the land,[34] is the scriptural touchstone concerning the twenty-ninth teaching of the church made prominent.

Role of the Holy Spirit in the Life of the Believer
Unit Two

Objective: The individual will demonstrate an understanding of the *doctrine* of the Church of God of Prophecy by describing the role of the Holy Spirit in the life of the believer, including the nature of Holy Spirit baptism, the role of speaking in tongues, the nature and functions of the gifts of the Spirit, and the significance of the fruit of the Spirit.

James Stone, *The Church of God of Prophecy History and Polity*, pp. 237-242

The baptism with the Holy Ghost, the next teaching, is the culminating experience in the order of salvation. The baptism of the Holy Ghost seals all of the other experiences. The Holy Spirit is not only the agency whereby man receives all of the experiences of salvation—the Holy Ghost convicts (John 16:7), the Holy Ghost brings forth the new birth (John 3:8), the Holy Spirit sanctifies the believer (Romans 15:16)—the Holy Spirit also empowers the sanctified believer by personally infilling the believer (1 Corinthians 6:19). This infilling of the Holy Spirit occurs in the experience of the baptism of the Holy Ghost.

The experience of the baptism of the Holy Spirit is first mentioned by John. "I indeed baptize you with water unto repentance: but he that cometh after me . . . he shall baptize you with the Holy Ghost" (Matthew 3:16). The baptizing agent for this experience is Jesus. The baptizing element—as water is the baptizing element for water baptism—is the Holy Spirit.

Although the Holy Ghost is the agency whereby all of the experience of salvation is received by the believer, the baptism of the Holy Ghost is distinct from these experiences. It was to people who were already believers in Christ that the Holy Spirit was promised (John 14). The sinner is not a candidate for the baptism of the Holy Ghost, for the baptism was promised to the believer. The promise of salvation is to the ungodly; the promise of the Holy Spirit is to those who are already in an experience of salvation.

The outpouring of the Holy Ghost in the history of the early church is characterized by at least three major distinctions. In the second, fourth, eighth, ninth, tenth, and nineteenth chapters of Acts, it can be ascertained that when the Holy Ghost was received, it was received in a spirit of worship by believers who then "spake in tongues." These three characteristics were always there: worship, believers, and speaking in tongues (further explained in later discussion). When the Holy Ghost comes into the temple of the worshiping believer, the individual will speak in tongues as the Spirit gives the utterance.

The Holy Ghost was promised to the church by Jesus, and on the day of Pentecost the Spirit came! "And suddenly there came a sound from heaven as of a rushing mighty wind, and it filled all the house where they were sitting. And there appeared unto them cloven tongues like as of fire, and it sat upon each of them. And they were all filled with the Holy Ghost, and began to speak with other tongues, as the Spirit gave them utterance" (Acts 2:2-4).

The Holy Spirit is now ever present to guide, to teach, to comfort, and to empower the believer by his indwelling.[35]

As indicated above, speaking in tongues is a phenomenon that accompanies the baptism of the Holy Ghost. Because of its prevalence in the scriptural account, the Church of God has come to accept *speaking in tongues as the evidence of the baptism of the Holy Ghost* in the believer's life. As Jesus stated "These signs shall follow them that believe . . .they shall speak with new tongues" (Mark 6:17). Wherever Jesus Christ has been preached and people believe, there should be speaking in tongues.[36] The reason why a person is sanctified is to be filled with the Holy Ghost.

From a close scrutiny of the recorded history of the church in the first century, the following facts can be ascertained. When the Holy Ghost fell on the day of Pentecost, the believers "began to speak with other tongues." The people gathered in Jerusalem on this special day were amazed that when these lowly disciples spoke, "every man heard them speak in his own language" (Acts 2:6). The disciples were speaking through the

Spirit a language they did not understand, but the people who heard them "heard them speak in their own language."

In Acts 4:31, the Scriptures indicate a somewhat similar outpouring of the Holy Ghost. Although there is no reference to speaking in tongues, this group was basically the same group as on the day of Pentecost and they, as a group, were accustomed to the evidence of the Holy Ghost. The absence of any reference to speaking in tongues does not discredit the argument. The filling of the Holy Ghost was the same as on the day of Pentecost, only smaller in scope.

After the Samaritans "had received the Word of God," Peter and John "prayed for them ,that they might receive the Holy Ghost" (Acts 8:14, 15). Although there is no reference again to them speaking in tongues, some kind of outward manifestation obviously occurred, for Simon, who had previously used sorcery to bewitch the people, immediately asked for the same power so he could lay his hands upon people and they would receive the Holy Ghost. The reaction of Simon definitely indicates an outward supernatural manifestation of some kind when the baptism of the Holy Ghost was received by the Samaritans.

In Acts 9:17, Paul receives, or at least receives the promise of, the baptism of the Holy Ghost. In this account there is again no indication of speaking in tongues; however, Paul was later to say, "I thank my God, I speak with tongues more than ye all" (1 Corinthians 14:18). The silence of any reference of speaking in tongues in this account is certainly no argument against tongues in view of Paul's later statement.

The Gentiles first received the baptism of the Holy Ghost in the house of Cornelius. As it was on the day of Pentecost to predominantly Jews, so it was on this day that the Holy Ghost was received by the Gentiles. As Luke records: "While Peter yet spake these words, the Holy Ghost fell on all them which heard the word. And they of the circumcision which believed were astonished, as many as came with Peter, because that on the Gentiles also was poured out the gift of the Holy Ghost. For they heard them speak with tongues, and magnify God" (Acts 10:44-46).

In the initial receiving of the baptism of the Holy Ghost for both the Jews and the Gentiles, the speaking in tongues is clearly indicated.

Finally, Paul, in witnessing to some disciples who had not heard about the Holy Ghost, preached to them this truth, and they received the baptism. Paul laid his hands upon them and "they spake with tongues and prophesied" (Acts 19:6). Again, the speaking of tongues is clearly recorded.

From the above Scriptures, the church has come to believe "speaking in tongues as the Spirit gives utterance is the initial, physical evidence of the baptism of the Holy Ghost."[37]

The early history of the church indicates that due to the indwelling of the Holy Ghost the church functioned with great power for several glorious years (Acts 4:32). The gifts and callings of the Spirit as illustrated in Paul's writings were in full operation for the edification of the church. These *gifts of the Spirit* were to be the means by which the church was to accomplish what it was intended to accomplish.

Since the "glory days" of the first century, the church has gone through several valleys of spiritual mediocrity. The Church of God of today, however, has come to believe that the church powerful in infancy will be the church powerful in full age. The gifts and callings ascertained from Romans 12:6-8, 1 Corinthians 12:28-30, and Ephesians 4:11,12 will once again be in full operation in the last-day's church as they were in the early church of the first century. The Church of God firmly believes in the *full restoration of the gifts.*

With the baptism of the Holy Ghost, the believer receives the source of spiritual power. When the believer proclaims the message of Jesus Christ, there are certain by-products of his salvation and message that just naturally follow. Jesus stated, "And these signs shall follow them that believe; In my name shall they cast out devils; they shall speak with new tongues; They shall take up serpents; and if they drink any deadly thing, it shall not hurt them; they shall lay hands on the sick, and they shall recover" (Mark 16:17, 18).

These signs will "follow the ministry of the Word until the work of the Church of God is finished and Jesus comes to receive [her] as His Bride."[38] These signs were manifested in the ministry of Jesus, in the ministry of the early church and in the ministry of the church today. The Church of God boldly stands for a manifestation of *signs following believers* today as they followed believers in the early church.

The power of the Holy Ghost in the life of the individual provides not only for signs to follow, but also for the ultimate fruition of the *fruit of the Spirit.* When a sinner is regenerated, the Holy Spirit implants the seed of salvation to come forth in the new birth. This seed of salvation must be cultivated through yielding to the Spirit until the crisis experiences of sanctification and the baptism of the Holy Ghost usher forth the full growth of the fruit of the Spirit.

The full growth of the fruit of the Spirit is love, joy, peace, long suffering, gentleness, goodness, faith, meekness, temperance.[39] These virtues are products of a Spirit-filled life. Jesus stated, "Beware of false prophets, which come to you in sheep's clothing, but inwardly they are ravening wolves. Ye shall know them by their fruit. Do men gather grapes of thorns, or figs of thistles? Even so every good tree bringeth forth good fruit; but a corrupt tree bringeth forth evil fruit. A good tree cannot bring forth evil fruit, neither can a corrupt tree bring forth good fruit" (Matthew 7:15-18).

The Spirit-filled, sanctified believer can bring forth nothing but the fruit of the Spirit. They are the distinguishing marks of the true disciple of Christ.

Divine healing has been one of the prominent teachings of the Church of God since the very beginning. The church has come to accept divine healing as meaning, "healing that is accomplished by the power of God."[40] The atonement through Jesus Christ provides not only salvation for mankind, but healing as well. As the Psalmist David proclaimed, "Bless the Lord, O my soul, and forget not all his benefits: Who forgiveth all thine iniquities; who healeth all thy diseases" (Psalms 103:2, 3).

The Gospels are literally full of accounts where Jesus performed healings during His earthly ministry. In the ministry of Jesus the blind received their sight, the speechless spoke, the withered limbs were restored, the lame walked, the mentally disturbed were clothed in their right mind, and the dead were even raised. Jesus actively fulfilled a healing ministry.

The Gospels also proclaim the healing ministry of the disciples. Jesus gave to them the power and the authority over all demons and all diseases (Luke 9). They went throughout the land preaching the gospel and healing the sick.

In the history of the early church after the ascension of Jesus, the ministry of healing is still evident for time and time again it is recorded where the sick were restored. Not only was healing through Jesus practiced, it was also taught. James stated, "Is any sick among you? let him call for the elders of the church; and let them pray over him, anointing him with oil in the name of the Lord: And the prayer of faith shall save the sick, and the Lord shall raise him up; and if he have committed sins, they shall be forgiven him. Confess your faults one to another, and pray one for another, that ye may be healed" (James 5:14-16). To the early church, the ministry of healing went hand in hand with the ministry of salvation.

The Church of God today stands firm on the teaching of divine healing. Peter stated, "Who his own self [Jesus] bare our sins in his own body on the tree, that we, being dead to sins, should live unto righteousness: by whose stripes ye were healed" (1 Peter 2:24). Since the church of the first century believed and practiced divine healing, the last-days Church of God is perfectly in order to preach divine healing and to teach it by precept and example.[41]

New Testament Ordinance

Unit Two

Objective: The individual will demonstrate an understanding of the *doctrine* of the Church of God of Prophecy by describing the significance of the New Testament ordinances of the Lord's supper, feet-washing, and water baptism and identifying the conditions under which they are observed.

Raymond M. Pruitt, *Fundamentals of the Faith*, pp. 364-370

The Christian faith holds that man is created in the image of God, and that, through His Spirit, he is able to commune with God. But he has no word adequate to describe what he experiences in these encounters with God, nor to explain the fellowship which he has with Christ and with other Christians. Yet these experiences are so vital and meaningful that he has a compelling desire to share them with others. It is in the act of sharing these deeper experiences that he gives witness to the truth that he is indeed made in the image of God, and that the presence of God in his life is real. The implication is clear that Christ will also be real in the lives of all who will be reconciled to Him through the finished work of Christ.

Although words cannot convey the essence of our relationships with God and with one another, there is a language for these experiences. It is the simple and beautiful language of signs and symbols, "those outward and visible forms through which is revealed the inward and invisible reality that moves and directs the soul of man."[42] Words are inadequate to express the deeper meanings, even in human relationships, to say nothing of those transcendent, indescribable experiences with God. For example, no word can express human love as well as the touch of a hand, the affectionate kiss, the light of the eyes, or the radiance of the face. These signs and symbols convey meanings and feelings which words alone cannot express. A single tear coursing down the cheek expresses sorrow better than ten thousand words. Human kindness is best expressed in acts of service and sacrifice to oneself (James 2:15,16; 1 John 3:17,18). The experiences of the soul and spirit are best expressed in the universal language of signs and symbols. The Lord has given the church such a means of expression in the ordinances, or sacraments, which He has instituted. The signs and symbols themselves do not impart spiritual grace, but are expressions of what has been imparted through our relationship with Christ.

Water Baptism

The Greek word for baptize is *baptizo* from the basic verb *bapto*, and it means "immerse, sink, submerge, to cover completely with the element used in baptism." None of the standard lexicons of the Greek language give "pour" or "sprinkle," nor can these terms be legitimately adduced from the Greek verb. Complete immersion is the New Testament mode of baptism (Luke 16:24; John 13:26; Revelation 19:13). Twice *baptizo* is translated "wash," and in both instances the thing washed was completely covered with water (Mark 7:4; Luke 11:38). Sprinkling does not symbolize the believer's total participation in Christ, which baptism is intended to signify.

Its significance. Water baptism signifies death, burial, and resurrection (Romans 6:1-4). As touching our salvation, it means that we die with Christ to sin, and through His death and resurrection, we are raised to life eternal. It means that we are baptized into Christ (immersed in Him), and that our new life is in Him (Galatians 3:27; Romans 6:3, 4). We were dead in trespasses and sins, but "he hath raised us up together, and made us sit together in heavenly places in Christ Jesus" (Ephesians 2:6). As touching our resurrection, baptism indicates that we share His victory over death. "But now is Christ risen from the dead, and become the firstfruits of them that slept. For since by man came death, by man came also the resurrection of the dead" (1 Corinthians 15:20, 21). The ordinance of baptism, then, is a symbol of the believer's identification with Christ in burial and resurrection (Romans 6:3, 4; Colossians 2:12; 1 Peter 3:21). Baptism replaces the Jewish circumcision which identified one with the people of God under the old covenant (Genesis 17:9-14; Colossians 2:10, 11). Baptism is the rite which identifies one with Christ (Romans 6:3-5).

The baptismal formula. The formula for water baptism was given by Jesus Himself: "Baptizing them in the name of the Father, and of the Son, and of the Holy Ghost" (Matthew 28:19). Peter did not contradict this directive of the Lord when he wrote in Acts 2:38 that penitents should "be baptized . . . in the name of Jesus Christ." Peter was not giving a formula for baptism, but was stating that those who are baptized are baptized into Christ. They are to live wholly unto Him, living and serving in His name. Also, Peter was emphasizing to the Jews that the only way to God was through Jesus. They knew of the Jewish proselyte baptisms, but Peter stressed that the only valid baptism is to be baptized into Christ. Actually, the literal meaning of Acts 2:38 is, "be baptized on the name of Jesus Christ." According to Thayer's Greek Lexicon, this means that the Jews were told to "repose their hope and confidence in His Messianic authority."[43]

The trinitarian formula signifies that those who are baptized are acknowledging that they have been immersed into spiritual communion with the Triune God. Of them it can be said, "The grace of the Lord Jesus Christ, and the love of God, and the communion of the Holy Ghost, [is] with you" (2 Corinthians 13:14).

The Lord's Supper

The Lord's Supper, or Holy Communion, was instituted by Jesus the night in which He was betrayed (Matthew 26:26-30; Mark 14:22-26; Luke 22:17-20).

Its significance. The Lord's Supper commemorates the death of Christ until He returns (Luke 22:19; 1 Corinthians 11: 23-26). It portrays the fact of redemption through the broken body and shed blood of Christ for us. It also symbolizes the believer's participation in the crucified Christ. In taking the Lord's Supper, believers do not merely look at the symbols, but receive them and feed upon them. Figuratively, they "eat the flesh of the Son of man, and drink his blood" (John 6:53), thus, demonstrating that they have appropriated the benefits of His sacrificial death. Communion also symbolizes the union of believers with one another in Christ. "The cup of blessing which we bless, is it not the communion of the blood of Christ? The bread which we break, is it not the communion of the body of Christ? For we being many are one bread, and one body: for we are all partakers of that one bread" (1 Corinthians 10:16, 17). As water baptism was substituted for circumcision, so the Lord's Supper superseded the Passover. Under the law, the Passover was the type of Christ's redemptive sacrifice. Since Christ Himself is the true Passover, a new rite was necessary to commemorate the death of the true Paschal Lamb.

The elements of the Lord's Supper. "The fruit of the vine" (Matthew 26:29) is the unfermented juice of the vine, not juice which has been allowed to ferment and change its character from the fresh product of the vine into something that could no longer be identified as being directly from the vine. No other kind of fruit juice is acceptable; it must be "of the vine." The bread is to be unleavened and broken (Exodus 12:39; Luke 22:13; 1 Corinthians 5:7, 8).

Much controversy has prevailed in the history of the doctrine of the Holy Communion regarding the words of Jesus when He said, "This is my body" (Matthew 26:26; Mark 14:22; Luke 22:19; 1 Corinthians 11:24). The Roman Catholics take a very literal view of those words and hold to the doctrine of transubstantiation, which means that when the bread and the wine are blessed, they become the very body and blood of Christ, and that each consecration is a new offering of Christ's sacrifice, and those who partake of the consecrated elements of the communion receive the saving and sanctifying grace from God. Of course, this view must be rejected for valid reasons: (1) If Jesus had meant the elements to be taken literally, there would have been two bodies of Christ present at the last supper—the Person offering the elements would have been one body, and the elements themselves would have been the other. (2) If the elements are the actual body of Christ, partaking of them smacks of cannibalism and is repugnant. (3) Such a notion also denies that Christ's offering of Himself on the cross was a once-for-all sacrifice for sin. The Catholic priest crucifies Him afresh at every mass. "Christ was once [for all] offered to bear the sins of many" (Hebrews 9:28). The Old Testament priests had to offer sacrifices over and over day after day (8:3; 9:25; 10:11); but the sacrifice of Christ was finished with that one offering of Himself (10:12, 14). We believe the Lord's Supper points back to the sacrifice of Christ, just as the Passover pointed forward to Him. The bread is the body of Christ just as the flesh of the passover lamb was His body.

Martin Luther and the Lutherans reject the doctrine of transubstantiation, and adopt the view of consubstantiation, which means that those who take the bread receive at the same time the body of the Lord in, under, and along with the bread, though the substance of both remains distinct from one another. This view is not far removed from the Catholic notion. If we receive the physical body of the Lord along with the bread in communion, then we imply the omnipresence of the physical body of Christ. Such an interpretation is totally foreign to Scripture and to reason. It also implies that material elements are essential to receiving Christ, and that makes salvation a matter of sacrament and ritual. Faith becomes unnecessary. This teaching is directly in conflict with the teaching of Christ in John 6:63: "It is the spirit that quickeneth; the flesh profiteth nothing: the words that I speak unto you, they are spirit, and they are life."

Those who may participate in the Lord's Supper. The Lord's Supper may be observed when there are at least two present (Acts 20:7; 1 Corinthians 11:18, 20, 22, 33, 34; Matthew 18:20.) The Scriptures do not provide any authority or example of its being observed by an individual.

Those who are guilty of sin are not permitted to observe the Lord's Supper (1 Corinthians 5:11), and those who partake unworthily "shall be guilty of the body and blood of the Lord" (11:27). Some, because they have partaken unworthily, have become sick, and some have died. To partake worthily is to receive it in faith, recognizing in one's heart the significance of this sacrament as it symbolizes for us Christ's sacrifice for our salvation, and the hope of His soon return to receive us to Himself.

Frequency of observance. The Scriptures nowhere give any specific number of times the Lord's Supper should be observed during the year. Jesus said, "For as often as ye eat this bread, and drink this cup, ye do shew the Lord's death till he come" (1 Corinthians 11:26). It could be done once a day, once a week, once a month, or once a quarter. Our churches are encouraged to observe the ordinance at least once each quarter.

Administration of the Lord's Supper.

There is no set order given in the New Testament as to whether participants should be seated at a table, kneeling at the altar, in the pews, or lined up to pass by the officiating minister. Therefore, the church rightly has made no rule, so long as the service has the dignity and sacredness which is appropriate for the Lord's Supper and all that it implies.

Feet-Washing.

On the last night that He was on earth in the flesh, and knowing full well what He would suffer in the coming hours, Jesus washed the feet of His disciples assembled for the last supper with Him. The account is given in John 13:2-17. When He had finished, He said to the disciples, "Ye call me Master and Lord: and ye say well; for so I am. If I then your Lord and Master, have washed your feet; ye also ought to wash one another's feet" (John 13:13, 14). The directive is just as clear as the injunction to observe the Lord's Supper. The early church evidently was faithful in the practice of washing feet, for some thirty years after Jesus instituted the ordinance, Paul, in setting down the qualifications for a certain order of elderly women in the church, stated, "Let not a widow be taken into the number under threescore years old, having been the wife of one man, Well reported of for good works; if she have brought up children, if she have lodged strangers, if she have washed the saint's feet, if she have relieved the afflicted, if she have diligently followed every good work" (1 Timothy 5:9, 10).

The New Testament teaching clearly requires the observance of feet-washing, and there always have been those who obeyed the clear command of the Lord Jesus; however the majority of Christians have not been faithful and obedient in this. They accept the command to observe the Lord's Supper, but try to explain away the equally explicit command to wash feet.

The significance of washing feet is seen in the words of Jesus, "If I then, your Lord and Master, have washed your feet; ye also ought to wash one another's feet." Elsewhere He said, "Whosoever will be chief among you, let him be your servant: Even as the Son of man came not to be ministered unto, but to minister, and to give his life a ransom for many" (Matthew 20:27, 18). As His disciples, we are to follow Him in ministering to the needs of others, not seeking the elevated positions of honor and prestige, but rather that we might serve. Love and humility are the key words to be remembered in relation to the ordinance of feet-washing (John 13:34, 35; Philippians 2:3-5).

Nature, Purpose and Functioning of the Church

Unit Two

Objective: The individual will demonstrate an understanding of the *doctrine* of the Church of God of Prophecy by explaining the nature, purpose, and function of the church.

Raymond M. Pruitt, *Fundamentals of the Faith*, pp. 348, 349, 363, 364

BACKGROUNDS, DEFINITIONS AND DISTINCTIONS

With so much confusion regarding the nature and role of the church in the religious world, it is important that we examine its meaning in the light of the Scriptures.

The Old Testament ecclesia. In the sense of being called out from among the other nations to be a holy people of God, Israel is called "the church in the wilderness" (Acts 7:38). God chose them (Deuteronomy 7:6-8) from the other nations and made them His covenant people, that they might witness to and evangelize the nations (Genesis 12:1-3; Romans 9:4, 5), receive and transmit the Scriptures (1 Peter 1:10-12; 2 Peter 1:19-21), and be the channel for the Redeemer (Genesis 49:10; Deuteronomy 18: 15-19; Isaiah 9:6, 7; Micah 5:1, 2; Luke 1:32; Romans 9:4, 5). But Israel was not a faithful people, and when the Messiah came, "He came unto his own, and his own received him not" (John 1:11). Because of their unfaithfulness, apostasy, and rejection of Christ, Israel was cut off, and the church was grafted into its place of mediatorial service (Romans 11:17-25). Their rejection is temporary, however, for Israel shall be restored (vv. 26-29).

The church is: called to be Christ's witnesses (Matthew 28:19, 20; Acts 1:8), "the pillar and ground of the truth" (1 Timothy 3:15), the body of Christ in the world (Ephesians

1:23). What Israel failed to do, the church is chosen to fulfill, and more.

The church is a new and unique entity. While the church replaces Israel in the place of mediatorial service, being grafted into the place where Israel had previously been called to serve, it is not a revised Israel, but is a new and unique entity, being conceived in the mind of God before the foundation of the world (Ephesians 1:3-5) and foretold by the prophets (Acts 15:14-17; Isaiah 11:10; 54:1-5; etc.). The church is composed mainly of Gentiles (Acts 15:14); its mission is to preach the gospel, to evangelize the world (Acts 1:8; Matthew 23:19, 20), and to prepare for the coming of the Lord (Titus 2:13,14).

The church differs from the kingdom. The fundamental idea of the kingdom is that of the rule of God established and acknowledged in the hearts of the people of God. "Thy kingdom come" is interpreted by the parallel petition, "Thy will be done in earth, as it is in heaven" (Matthew 6:10). The kingdom is both inward and outward. It is essentially inward, being primarily a relationship of loving submission to God. To the Pharisees, who are looking for the kingdom, Jesus said: "The kingdom of God is within you" (Luke 17:21). "The word of the kingdom . . . which was sown in his heart" (Matthew 13:19). "The kingdom of heaven is like unto leaven, which a woman took, and hid in the three measures of meal, till the whole was leavened" (Matthew 13:33).

The outward expression of the kingdom is seen in the transformation of social institutions, such as the family, state, economic order, and such, as they are influenced by the righteous character of godly men and women.

The church is itself an outward expression of the kingdom of God. When Jesus established His church, it was that it would be the institution whose task would be to help bring about the rule of God in the hearts of men. The kingdom is a wider concept than the last-days institution whose direct vocation is to bear witness for Christ and His truth to men, to preach and spread the gospel of the kingdom in all of its fullness, to maintain God's worship, to administer all of the sacraments, to provide for the edification and equipment of its membership, and to work for the unity of God's people everywhere. One is a citizen of the kingdom, but he belongs to the church by membership.

There is also, of course, an invisible relationship which true members have with the church. In addition to the visible and extrinsic relations of receiving the membership covenant, being placed on the church roll book, and participating in the activities of the church, its members are also intrinsically placed in the body by the Holy Spirit (1 Corinthians 12:13,18), and this level of membership is experienced both in spiritual communion with Christ, who is the Head of the church, and through love and Christian fellowship with the members of His body, the church.

There is no tension between the church and the kingdom, for they are interdependent. The church is within the kingdom and seeks to enlarge it by bringing others to Christ. But the kingdom and the church are not one and the same. One may be in the kingdom without being in the church. Conversely, an individual may be on the church membership roll and not be in the Kingdom.

THE FUNCTION OF THE CHURCH

So long as the early church was one undivided body as Christ ordained it to be, there was little need to formally define the distinguishing marks of the true church. But as heresies arose, dividing the church, it became necessary to more deliberately define its purpose and function in the world. Clearly, there is a pattern which the church must fit if it is to fulfill its role as the body of Christ. Listed below are some of the elements of its identity:

1. It must preach the pure Word of God. "If ye continue in my word, then are ye my disciples indeed . . . He that is of God heareth God's words" (John 8:31, 47). "Whosoever transgresseth, and abideth not in the doctrine of Christ, hath not God. He that abideth in the doctrine of Christ, he hath both the Father and the Son" (2 John 9). See also John 14: 23; 1 John 4:1-3.

2. It must properly administer all of the ordinances. They are: water baptism (Matthew 28:19; Mark 16:15, 16), the Lord's Supper (1 Corinthians 11:23-30), and the washing of the saints' feet (John 13:2-17).

3. It must faithfully exercise discipline (Matthew 18:18; 1 Corinthians 5:1-5, 13; 14:33, 40; Revelation 2:14, 15, 20).

4. It must be a church of love. "A new commandment I give unto you, That ye love one another; as I have loved you, that

ye also love one another. By this shall all men know that ye are my disciples, if ye have love one to another" (John 13:34, 35; 1 John 4:7-21).

5. Its polity and administration must be in harmony with the New Testament pattern (1 Corinthians 12:28; Ephesians 4:11-16).

6. It must exercise the spiritual gifts which were set in the Church by God (1 Corinthians 12; Ephesians 4).

7. It must be faithful in carrying out its divinely appointed mission in the world, which is a complex and many-sided role:

- It must glorify God in all things (Romans 15:6, 9; Ephesians 1:5, 6, 12, 14, 18; 3:21; 2 Thessalonians 1:12; 1 Peter 4:11).
- It must edify the flock (Ephesians 4:11-16; Colossians 2:7; 1 Corinthians 14: 26; Jude 20; 1 Corinthians 3:10-15).
- It must purify itself (Ephesians 5:26, 27; John 15:2; Hebrews 12:10; 1 Corinthians 11:32; 11:28-31; 2 Corinthians 7:1; 1 John 3:23; Acts 5:11; Matthew 18:17; 1 Corinthians 5:6-8, 13; Romans 16:17; 2 Thessalonians 3:6, 14; Titus 3:10, 11; 2 John 10).
- It must teach all things which Jesus commanded (Matthew 28:19; Ephesians 4:11, 12; Philippians 4:8).
- It must evangelize the world (Matthew 28:19; Mark 16:15; Luke 24:46-48; Acts 1:8; 2:41-47).
- It must be an enlightening and restraining influence in the world (Matthew 5:13-16; 2 Thessalonians 2:6, 7; Genesis 18:22-33).
- It must promote all that is good and oppose all that is evil (Galatians 6:10; Acts 10:38-43; Romans 12:9).

Objective: The individual will demonstrate an understanding of the *doctrine* of the Church of God of Prophecy by explaining the position of the Church of God of Prophecy regarding the last things including the significance of the premillennial second coming of Christ, the resurrection of the dead, and eternal rewards.

James Stone, *The Church of God of Prophecy History and Polity*, pp. 246-249

The term *eschatology* comes from those passages of Scripture which deal with "the last days," "these last times," and "the last time."[44] Those passages of Scripture (respectively Isaiah 2:2, 1 Peter 1:20, and 1 John 2:18) speak of a time to come—the last time. The Greek word translated "last" is *eschatos* (es-khat-os). Thus, eschatology is the study of last things.

The last things of importance here are, *the premillennial second coming of Jesus, the resurrection, the eternal life for the righteous and the eternal punishment for the wicked.* The church is anxiously awaiting the fulfilling of these events. They are the end of which the race was begun.

Luke penned the words of the two men in white apparel as they spoke to the disciples who were steadfastly looking toward heaven as Jesus ascended, "Ye men of Galilee, why stand ye gazing up into heaven?" Then went on to say, "This same Jesus, which is taken up from you into heaven, shall so come in like manner as ye have seen him go into heaven" (Acts 1:11). The Lord Jesus is coming again. The second coming of Christ "has been one of the prominent teachings of the Church of God from the very beginning."[45]

The Word of God clearly proclaims the second coming of Jesus. There is a strong emphasis on the Second Coming throughout the New Testament. Jesus Himself referred to His return in the last of His earthly ministry (Matthew 24:30; 25:31; 26:64; John 14:3). As stated above, Acts 1:11 predicts His return. The apostles and writers of the New Testament refer to the Second Coming numerous times (Acts 3:20, 21; Philippians 3:20; 1 Thessalonians 4:15, 16; 2 Thessalonians 1:7, 10; Titus 2:13; Hebrews 9:28). Without doubt, the second coming of Christ is a biblical fact.

The Scriptures not only state that Jesus will return, the Word of God also proclaims certain facts about His return. Some of those basic facts are His coming will be premillennial (Revelation 20:6); His coming will be a personal coming (Acts 1:11); His coming will be a physical coming (Acts 1:11); His coming will be a visible coming (Revelation 1:7); His coming will be a sudden coming (Matthew 24:42, 44); and His coming will be a triumphant coming (Matthew 24:30). The coming Son of man will personally, physically, visibly, suddenly return in triumphant glory. The second coming of Jesus has and always will be a prominent teaching of the Church of God.

Along with the second coming of Christ will be the first resurrection of the dead. Paul boldly stated the teaching of the resurrection in 1 Corinthians 15:12, 20-22. He taught, "Now if Christ be preached that he rose from the dead, how say some among you that there is no resurrection of the dead? . . . But now is Christ risen from the dead, and become the firstfruits of them that slept. For since by man came death, by man came also the resurrection of the dead. For as in Adam all die, even so in Christ shall all be made alive."

The Church of God stands firm on this vital doctrine and "teaches the resurrection exactly as it is taught in the New Testament."[46]

There are, in fact, two resurrections of the dead. In the earlier stage of the second coming of Jesus, the dead in Christ will be resurrected. Paul states, "For the Lord himself shall descend from heaven with a shout, with the voice of the archangel, and with the trump of God: and the dead in Christ shall rise first: then we which are alive and remain shall be caught up together with them in the clouds, to meet the Lord in the air: and so shall we ever be with the Lord" (1 Thessalonians 4:16, 17).

The initial aspect of the second coming of Christ will consist of the coming of Christ for His saints. The dead in Christ shall arise (the first resurrection), the living saints shall be changed, and together they will rise to meet Jesus in the air.[47] It is difficult to ascertain just what will happen after the first resurrection and the rapture.[48] From the Scriptures there is an indication of the "marriage of the Lamb" (Revelation 19:7) and a "marriage supper" (Revelation 19:9). The "marriage" will evidently be between the Lamb and the "bride of Christ" (Revelation 21:9). After the supper, the last aspect of the second coming of Christ will begin with the coming of Christ with His saints in full view of the world.

The single event of the second coming of Christ consists of all that transpires between the initial coming for His saints and ultimate coming with His saints. Jesus Christ returning to earth after the marriage supper with all of His saints will then establish the visible, the realized, the perfected kingdom of God on earth.[49] The saints shall rule and "reign with him [Christ] a thousand years" (Revelation 20:6).

The dead in Christ, after the first resurrection, will reign with the transfigured saints of the rapture for one thousand years (vv. 4, 6). The first resurrection of Revelation 20:6, however, will not be the only resurrection, for Revelation 20:5 states, "But the rest of the dead lived not again until the thousand years were finished." There will also be a resurrection of the unjust. As Paul proclaims, "there shall be a resurrection of the dead, both of the just and unjust" (Acts 24:15). John clinches the argument by stating, "Marvel not at this: for the hour is coming, in the which all that are in the graves shall hear his voice, and shall come forth; they that have done good, unto the resurrection of life; and they that have done evil, unto the resurrection of damnation" (John 5:28, 29).

The Church of God holds to the belief in two resurrections. The church bases that belief on the Word of God, for the Bible proclaims that there will be two resurrections. The church's stand on the resurrection is summarized as "the righteous will be resurrected at the coming of the Lord, and a thousand years later, after the millennial reign in which these righteous saints will participate, the wicked dead shall be raised and eternal judgment will be pronounced upon them."[50]

The next two teachings of the church and the last two dealing with eschatology are eternal life for the righteous and eternal punishment for the wicked. These two teachings are also richly supported by the Scriptures. Some of those scriptures are eternal life for the righteous (Matthew 25:46; Luke 18:30; John 10:28; Romans 6:22; 1 John 5:11-13); eternal punishment for the wicked (Matthew 24:5; 25:30, 41, 46, Luke 16:19-31; Revelation 20:15). The Word of God certainly supports the fact that whatever man does in this life he will be judged accordingly for the life to come.

NOTES

[1] *Minutes* of the sixty-fifth annual Assembly of the Church of God of Prophecy, 1970, p. 121.

[2] From *A Guide to the Thought of St. Augustine*, Eugene Portalie (Chicago: Regnery, 1960).

[3] From *The Creeds of Christendom*, Philip Schaff (New York: Harper & Bros., 1932), II: 66-70.

[4] *Minutes*, 1970, *op. cit.*

[5] From *Body of Divinity*, John Gill (Grand Rapids: Baker, 1951).

[6] From *Church History in Plain Language*, Bruce L. Shelley (Waco, TX: Word Books, 1982), p. 128.

[7] Schaff, *op. cit.*

[8] From *Word Studies in the New Testament*, Marvin R. Vincent (Grand Rapids: Eerdmans, 1957).

[9] From *Introductory Lectures in Systematic Theology*, Henry C. Thiessen (Grand Rapids: Eerdmans, 1949), p. 143.

[10] From *The Person of Christ*, Philip Schaff (Garden City, NY: Doubleday, 1924).

[11] From *Basic Bible Beliefs*, M. A. Tomlinson (Cleveland, TN: White Wing Publishing House, 1961), p. 6.

[12] *Ibid.*, p. 7.

[13] *Ibid.*, p. 12.

[14] From *A Critical Lexicon and Concordance*, Ethelbert W. Bullinger (Grand Rapids: Zondervan, 1975), p. 379.

[15] M. A. Tomlinson, *op. cit.*, p. 14.

[16] *Ibid.*

[17] *Ibid.*, p. 65.

[18] Bible Training Institute, *Text* (Cleveland, TN: White Wing, 1976), I: 44.

[19] *Ibid.*, p. 21.

[20] M. A. Tomlinson, *op. cit.*, p. 71.

[21] *Ibid.*, p. 107.

[22] *Ibid.*, p. 110.

[23] *Ibid.*, p. 105.

[24] *Ibid.*, p. 104.

[25] *Ibid.*, p. 121.

[26] *Ibid.*

[27] *Ibid.*, p. 122.

[28] From *The Gospel of Matthew*, William Barclay (Philadelphia: Westminster, 1956), I:148.

[29] *Ibid.*, p. 151.

[30]*Ibid.*, p. 154.

[31]*Ibid.*, p. 149.

[32]M. A. Tomlinson, *op. cit.*, p. 125.

[33]*Ibid.*, p. 125.

[34]*Ibid.*, p. 127; *Church of God of Prophecy Business Guide* (Cleveland, TN: White Wing, 1989), pp. 37, 38.

[35]M. A. Tomlinson, *op. cit.*, p. 28.

[36]*Ibid.*, p. 29; Vinson Synan, *The Twentieth-Century Pentecostal Explosion* (Altamonte Springs, FL: Creation, 1987).

[37]"Twenty-nine Important Bible Truths" (Cleveland, TN: White Wing, 1976), p. 5.

[38]M. A. Tomlinson, *op. cit.*, p. 40.

[39]*Ibid.*, p. 47.

[40]*Ibid.*, p. 49.

[41]*Ibid.*

[42]From *Signs and Symbols in Christian Art*, George Ferguson (New York: Oxford University, 1958), p. iii.

[43]From *A Greek-English Lexicon of the New Testament*, J. H. Thayer (New York: American, 1886).

[44]From *Systematic Theology*, L. Berkhof (Grand Rapids: Wm. B. Eerdmans, 1969), p. 666.

[45]M. A. Tomlinson, *op. cit.*, p. 71.

[46]*Ibid.*, p. 79.

[47]*Ibid.*, p. 81.

[48]*Ibid.*

[49]*Ibid.*

[50]*Ibid.*, p. 82.

FOUNDATIONS COURSE: A Concise History/Doctrine

Registration Form for: Ministers,
Ministerial Candidates,
and Certified Teacher Candidates

Name : _____

Address: _____

_____

Local Church: _____

Pastor: _____

In order to earn a Certificate of Completion or Leadership Development Unit the ministerial candidate should register with the state/regional/national office. The following criteria must be met:

- The ministerial candidate must be approved by the Overseer.
- The ministerial participant must complete the course of study in a reasonable time.
- The approved CBL text must be read and the accompanying examination and assignments successfully completed with a score of 95% (open-book test). The Examination should be sent to the state/regional/national office for grading.

I am a candidate for:
❐ Minister's License   ❐ Minister Upgrading
❐ Certified Teacher

Please indicate which of the following you are requesting credit for:
❐ LDU Credit
❐ Leadership Certificate
❐ Advanced Leadership Certificate
❐ State/Regional Credit

Date _____   Grade _____

Applicant Signature: _____